God,
I See You

In the Valley of the Unknown

Dr. Cindy H. Carr, D.Min., MACL

This book is published by **CHC Connect**.

All views and opinions expressed in this work are those of the author. Any errors or omissions are unintentional.

Printed in the United States of America
First Edition, 2026

ISBN: 978-1-971192-23-9

For permissions or inquiries, contact:
Cindy H. Carr
cindyhcarr@outlook.com
www.cindyhcarr.com

How to Use This Book

This devotional is written for everyday people walking through real valleys—seasons of loss, uncertainty, disappointment, confusion, and rebuilding.

Each chapter includes:
• A brief orientation ("This chapter explores…") so you can quickly find the valley you're in.
• A first-person biblical narrative designed to help you locate yourself in the story.
• A Gentle Truth—one clear takeaway to carry with you.
• A Small Practice—one simple step you can try today.

Read one chapter per day, one chapter per week, or revisit chapters as needed. If you are in an intense season of grief, trauma, or clinical distress, consider reading with a trusted friend, pastor, or licensed counselor.

Note: The first-person chapters are imaginative retellings rooted in Scripture, written to help you locate your life in God's story. They are not presented as verbatim biblical quotations.

Dedication

This book is dedicated to all who long to go deeper than the words on the page—to those who desire to step into the biblical experience and imagine what it may have felt like to walk in those ancient days.

Each chapter is written as a message from one who lived the story firsthand. While artistic liberties have been taken to invite the reader into the moment, the biblical narrative is followed as closely and faithfully as possible.

May these pages help you see, feel, and encounter the story—and the God within it—in a more personal way.

Acknowledgements

I want to thank the people who have walked beside me through both visible and unseen valleys. Your prayers, encouragement, and quiet faithfulness sustained me more than you know. Thank you for holding space for questions, for truth, and for hope.

To those who read early drafts, offered thoughtful feedback, or spoke words of encouragement at just the right moment—your generosity shaped this book in ways that go far beyond the words on these pages.

I am grateful for every church and seminary that makes room for contemplative, imaginative engagement with Scripture—places where Scripture is not only studied, but inhabited, prayed, and experienced with reverence and creativity.

I am especially thankful to those who trusted me with their stories, their questions, and their pain. You reminded me why this work matters.

And to every reader who finds themselves somewhere in the valley of the unknown: thank you for your courage to keep walking. May you know that you are seen, held, and never alone.

Table of Contents

Chapter One

When the Fire Dies Down

This chapter explores Peter—
for anyone who feels the fire of fear and shame,
and needs mercy that meets you before you can explain yourself.

I never imagined it would happen this way.

Not after everything I had seen.
Not after everything I had promised.

The night air was cold, sharper than I expected. The kind of cold that slips under your cloak and settles into your bones. I stood close to the fire, not because I wanted the warmth, but because I didn't want to be alone with my thoughts.

Someone asked me a question.

It wasn't loud.
It wasn't angry.
It wasn't even meant to corner me.

Just a question.

"Weren't you with Him?"

My heart raced before my mind could catch up. The words came out faster than I could stop them.

"No."

I don't even remember exactly how I said it. I just know it wasn't true.

The fire crackled. Someone laughed nearby. Life kept moving as if nothing monumental had just happened. But inside me, something split open.

I had sworn I would never do this.

I had meant it when I said I would follow Him anywhere. I had believed it when I promised I would stand firm. I wasn't lying when I spoke those words back then. I just didn't know how thin courage becomes when fear takes over your body.

Another question came.
Then another.

Each time, my answer came easier.

"No."
"I don't know Him."
"That's not me."

With every word, I felt myself drifting farther from the One I loved most. Not because He moved—but because I did.

When it was over, I walked away from the fire.

The warmth faded quickly. The night felt even colder. And somewhere in the distance, a sound broke through the dark—sharp, sudden, unmistakable.

I stopped.

Because I remembered something He had said.

I remembered the look in His eyes when He said it—not accusing, not dramatic. Just honest. Just knowing.

And suddenly I couldn't stand upright anymore.

I had followed Him so closely once. I had felt so sure. So alive. So chosen. I had heard His voice clearly—felt guided, protected, seen.

And now?

Now I felt like I had lost Him completely.

Not because I stopped believing.
Not because I wanted to walk away.
But because fear had undone me.

Maybe you know this place.

The place where you didn't intend to lose your way—but here you are anyway. Where the fire you once felt has cooled. Where confidence has given way to confusion. Where you still love God, but you don't know how you ended up so far from where you thought you'd be.

Sometimes the valley comes through failure.
Sometimes through shame.
Sometimes through fear that overwhelms the body before the soul can speak.

In that place, God can feel silent.

Distant.

Gone.

I wept that night. Not quiet tears. The kind that come from deep inside your chest. The kind that carry regret, grief, and disbelief all at once.

I thought I was finished.

I thought I had disqualified myself.

But I didn't know yet that love doesn't disappear when you fall apart. That grace doesn't turn its back when courage fails. That the One who called me knew exactly how human I was when He did.

I didn't know yet that the story wasn't over.

Not even close.

The Gentle Truth

There are moments in life when we look back and wonder how we drifted so far from what once felt certain. When fear overrides faith. When our nervous systems react before our hearts can steady themselves.

When shame whispers that we've ruined everything.

But distance does not mean abandonment.

God's presence is not erased by your worst moment. His love does not hinge on your strongest resolve. And the valley you're walking through is not proof that you've lost Him—it may be the place where grace meets you most tenderly.

A Small Practice for the Valley

If you feel distant from God right now, try this simple prayer—out loud if you can:

"God, I am here.
I don't know how I got here.
But I am still reaching for You."

No explanations.
No fixing.
Just honesty.

Chapter Two

If You Had Been Here

This chapter explores Martha—
for anyone grieving what should not have been,
and needs hope while waiting for resurrection.

The house was full, but it felt empty.

People came in soft waves—quiet voices, careful footsteps, arms full of food no one really wanted. They meant well. I know they did. But grief has a way of making kindness feel like noise.

I watched their mouths move. I heard the sound of comfort. I nodded at all the right moments. I even thanked them.

And inside, I kept thinking the same thing:

Where is He?

Not in the way people ask when they've never believed.
In the way believers ask when something sacred has been taken.

I had sent for Him.

That part matters.

I didn't just hope He'd come. I didn't just whisper a prayer into the ceiling and wait for the universe to respond. I sent a message. I reached out. I made it clear.

The one You love is sick.

And I believed—truly believed—He would come.

Because I had seen Him come before.

I had watched Him stop for people no one else would stop for. I had watched Him touch what others avoided. I had watched Him speak, and impossible things became possible. I had heard hope in His voice so many times that hope felt like a certainty.

So when my brother got worse, I wasn't afraid in the beginning.

I thought: Any minute now.

He'll come down the road.
He'll step into the doorway.
He'll say the words.
He'll do what He does.

And then… He didn't.

The hours stretched out like a rope that kept slipping through my hands.

The fever rose. The breathing changed. The panic came in little flashes—quick and sharp—followed by long, helpless watching. I pressed cool cloths to his forehead. I begged quietly while no one was listening. I listened for footsteps outside.

And nothing.

Not even a message.

No word.
No warning.
No explanation.

I told myself not to assume the worst. I reminded myself that He loved us. I argued with my own heart, the way people do when they're trying to keep faith from collapsing.

But then my brother's body did what bodies do when life leaves.

It went still.

And the world changed in one breath.

The grief arrived first—heavy and wild. Then came something else—something I didn't want to admit because it felt unholy.

Disappointment.

Not in a vague way. Not in a philosophical way.

In a personal way.

I kept thinking:

He could have stopped this.

And then I thought the sentence that made my throat tighten with anger and my chest tighten with sorrow:

If You had been here…

Not because I stopped believing He could.
But because I could not understand why He didn't.

People say strange things when they are grieving. They talk about purpose. They talk about mysterious plans. They talk about Heaven like it erases the empty chair at the table.

But grief doesn't work that way.

Grief is not impressed by good theology.

Grief is a wound.

And my wound had a question inside it.

Where were You?

I heard He had finally come.

Not to the house.

Not to the bedside.

To the road outside the village—as if arriving late had become its own kind of arrival.

I don't know what I expected to feel when I heard. Relief? Gratitude? Peace?

I didn't feel any of those things.

I felt the same thing I had felt for days:

A storm I could not control.

So I went out to meet Him.

And the moment I saw Him, the sentence erupted before I could swallow it:

"If You had been here… he wouldn't have died."

There it was. My honest faith. My honest disappointment. My sorrow and my accusation braided together in one breath.

He didn't flinch.

That's what I remember most.

He didn't scold me for my tone.
He didn't correct my emotions.
He didn't tighten His face as if I had offended Him.

He looked at me like someone who had already carried my grief before I said a word.

And He spoke—not as someone defending Himself, but as someone steady enough to hold me while I shook.

I tried to keep it together. I tried to talk like a person who still believed the right things. I said what I knew to say.

But knowing is different than feeling.

You can recite hope and still be drowning.

You can believe God is good and still feel abandoned.

You can love God and still say, “This shouldn’t have happened.”

And He let me say it.

Then came the walk to the tomb.

A stone. A sealed place. The finality of it.

Someone told Him what He already knew: the smell would be awful. The time had passed. The outcome was set.

Because we think once something is sealed, God is too late.

But He stood there like timing was not His enemy.

And then—this part still undoes me—He wept.

He didn't only bring power.

He brought tears.

As if to say: I am not above your grief. I am with you in it.

His tears didn't mean He couldn't change anything. His tears meant love was not detached.

And then He spoke into the sealed place like death was only a door.

And what I thought was over… wasn't.

When Resurrection Is Still Ahead

I know how this story ends.

That matters.

My brother walked out of the grave. I held his face again. I heard his voice. I watched life return where death had ruled.

Not everyone gets to witness resurrection that quickly.

Most grief does not resolve in front of a crowd.
Most losses are not undone before our eyes.
Most goodbyes are not followed by immediate reunion.

And that waiting—between loss and restoration—can feel unbearable.

We live inside time.
Inside days that stretch long and heavy.
Inside nights where absence echoes louder than hope.

But God does not experience time the way we do.

What feels endless to us is held differently by Him.

Scripture tells us that resurrection is not only a moment—it is a promise. One that will come for all who love Him. One that will reunite what death has separated. One that will arrive not late, but right on time—even if it feels delayed now.

For those still waiting, this matters:

Your grief is not proof that the resurrection has failed.
Your sorrow is not evidence that hope is gone.
And your waiting is not forgotten.

The reunion you long for will come.

And when it does, it will feel like the blink of an eye.

And as we wait, we must remember that we are all

one family in heaven and on earth. (See 1 Corinthians 15:52; Ephesians 3:15.)

The Gentle Truth

There are seasons when we believe God could have prevented something, and we cannot understand why He didn't.

And that confusion can feel like distance.

But God's closeness is not measured by how quickly He fixes what we fear. Sometimes He arrives in a way that confronts our assumptions, not our worth.

You are allowed to grieve.
You are allowed to be disappointed.
You are allowed to say, "If You had been here…"

And still be loved.

God is not fragile. Your honesty will not scare Him away.

A Small Practice for the Valley

If you're grieving—or if you're disappointed with God's timing—pray this without editing yourself:

"God, I miss what I lost.
I don't understand the delay.
I still want You.
Meet me here."

Then do one small thing that honors your humanity today:
drink water, take a shower, step outside (if that's accessible), reach out to one safe person, or simply rest without guilt.

Chapter Three

The Shortcut

**This chapter explores Sarah—
for anyone tempted to take life into their own hands, and needs to trust that God is still writing the story.**

I used to think waiting was a spiritual gift.

Now I know it can also be a spiritual wound.

At first, I waited with hope. The kind of hope that feels clean. Certain. Bright. I believed the promise the way you believe sunrise is coming—because you've seen it come before.

But years have a way of grinding down even the best beginnings.

One month becomes twelve.
One year becomes ten.
And eventually the calendar starts to feel like it's mocking you.

Every time someone announced a pregnancy, something inside me tightened. Every time I heard laughter in the next tent, I wondered what it would feel like to laugh again without bitterness hiding in the sound.

I prayed.
I trusted.
I tried to be patient.

And then patience started to feel like pretending.

Because I still loved God, but I couldn't see Him anymore—not in the way I used to. The promise felt like a story I told myself to make the days bearable. And the silence… the silence felt like abandonment.

Not the kind where you stop believing.
The kind where you keep believing and still feel alone.

So I did what people do when the waiting gets unbearable.

I took control.

At first, it felt logical—like wisdom. Like "helping God." Like I was simply taking initiative in the space where Heaven was apparently taking its time.

I told myself I wasn't losing faith. I was being practical.

But faith and fear can sound very similar when you're desperate.

I didn't realize I was building a shortcut that would become someone else's wilderness.

I can't explain the reasoning without admitting the truth beneath it: I was tired of feeling powerless.

Waiting had made me feel small. Invisible. Like my life was happening to me instead of through me.

So I found a way to make something happen.

I convinced myself it would be fine.

I told myself it wouldn't hurt anyone.

I told myself, God will still keep His promise. This is just how it has to happen.

But there's a thing about taking matters into your own hands—especially when you're hurting:

You rarely hold only your own life in the process.

You start moving people around like pieces on a board because you're trying to outrun disappointment. You turn human hearts into solutions. You call it strategy, but it's really desperation dressed in confidence.

And when the plan started working—when I saw evidence that something was finally moving forward—there was a moment I felt relief.

Finally.

Something.

Anything.

But relief can turn sour fast when it's built on fear.

Because once the outcome was secured, another emotion came in behind it—sharp and ugly, like a thorn you can't pull out.

Jealousy.

I hated that it was there. I hated that it was mine. I hated the way it rose up in my throat when I saw the proof of what I couldn't do.

And then the house—my house—filled with tension. Not because of one cruel act, but because of the slow accumulation of wounded people living too close together.

Every look felt loaded.
Every conversation felt like a test.
Every silence felt like accusation.

And I began doing what wounded people do when they can't tolerate what they've created:

I blamed the person caught in the middle.

Not the promise.
Not the pressure.
Not the fear.

The person.

And I watched my own heart harden.

That's the part no one wants to say out loud: Sometimes the mess we make doesn't just change the situation—it changes us.

It makes us harsher.
More defensive.
Less gentle.

And the farther you drift from gentleness, the farther God can feel.

Not because He moved.

Because shame builds walls. And I was laying brick by brick.

Then God came.

Not with thunder.
Not with scolding.
Not with the tone of someone disappointed that I didn't "wait correctly."

He came close.

And He spoke promise again—as if my shortcut hadn't erased His plan.

As if my panic hadn't canceled His faithfulness.

As if my mess didn't surprise Him.

It should have settled me. It should have made me breathe.

But sometimes, when God speaks kindness to a guilty heart, it doesn't feel comforting at first.

It feels exposing.

Because now you have to face the truth: you weren't abandoned. You were afraid.

And you weren't forgotten. You were tired.

And you weren't powerless. You were human.

I thought the story would end with God fixing everything neatly.

But real life doesn't always wrap up with a bow.

Sometimes God's mercy comes in the form of provision inside the consequences.

Because the child was born.

And when he cried, I felt something strange—joy mixed with grief, relief mixed with regret. Life had come from my attempt to outrun waiting, and I didn't know what to do with the weight of that.

And the harder part?

I wasn't the only one affected.

Someone else's life had been turned upside down because of my fear.

Someone else carried the cost of my "solution."

Someone else's body, safety, and future had been caught in the blast radius of my impatience.

I had made a mess.

And it didn't just touch me.

If you've ever been there—if you've ever made things worse because you were desperate for relief—hear this gently:

God is not caught off guard by your shortcuts.

That does not mean shortcuts are harmless.
It means God's compassion reaches farther than your failure.

He can meet you in what you regret.
He can redeem what you cannot undo.
He can provide for the lives impacted by your choices.

God is not limited to perfect stories.

He is present even when you're ashamed of your chapter.

The Gentle Truth

When God feels late, we are tempted to force outcomes. We speed up, control, manipulate, scramble—anything to escape uncertainty.

But the valley does not mean God is gone.

Even when you took it into your own hands, God was not surprised. Even when you made a mess, God was not defeated. Even when your fear harmed something precious, God's compassion did not run out.

He can hold your regret without crushing you.

And He can move toward everyone involved—not just the one who "got it wrong."

A Small Practice for the Valley

If you feel like you've made things worse, pray this without hiding:

"God, I tried to fix what I couldn't control.
I'm sorry for what I've damaged.
Show me the next right step.
And be kind to everyone I've affected."

Then take one small step of repair:

- tell the truth to one safe person,
- make one humble apology,
- ask for wisdom before you act again,
- or choose one quiet day of waiting without forcing anything.

Chapter Four

Seen in the Wilderness

This chapter explores Hagar—
for anyone who feels abandoned, displaced, or unseen, and needs to know God finds people in the wilderness.

I didn't choose to be part of their plan.

That's the first thing you should know.

My life was already small in the eyes of those who owned it. I belonged to someone else's household, someone else's schedule, someone else's future. My name was spoken when I was needed and forgotten when I wasn't.

Then I became an answer.

Not a person—an answer.

A solution to a promise that felt too slow.

They spoke about faith and legacy and what God had said, and I stood there listening, realizing none of it was really about me. It was about their fear of waiting. Their fear of disappointment. Their fear that God had gone quiet and maybe wasn't coming through.

And suddenly my body was part of their desperation.

I don't tell you that to make you angry at them—though you might be. I tell you because this is how so many people enter the valley of the unknown: not by choosing it, but by being pulled into someone else's storm.

At first, I tried to survive it the way you survive anything you cannot change—by staying small.

Say the right words.
Do what you're told.
Don't make trouble.
Don't hope too loud.

But hope has a way of rising anyway.

And when life began to grow inside me, I felt something I hadn't felt in a long time.

Worth.

Not because I had earned it. Because something in me whispered, suddenly, that I mattered. That I was seen. That my story was real even if it lived in the shadows of someone else's tent.

That whisper didn't last.

Because the moment my condition became visible, the household shifted.

It wasn't just tension. It was heat.

There were looks that burned.
Silences that accused.
Words that landed like stones.

I was the same person, but I had become a problem.

And when wounded people start to regret what they rushed into, they look for someone to blame.

They did not blame the fear that drove them.
They did not blame the impatience.
They did not blame the plan.

They blamed me.

And the harshness grew until I couldn't breathe in my own life.

So I ran.

I didn't run with a map. I ran with instinct.

Pregnant. Alone. Vulnerable.

The wilderness was not poetic to me. It wasn't a metaphor. It was danger.

It was the place where survival decisions are made with shaking hands.

I remember the sun. The way it pressed down like weight.
I remember my mouth—dry, cracking.

I remember the sound of my own breathing getting faster, then smaller, then almost gone.

And in that wilderness, a question rose in me like prayer and accusation mixed together:

Does God see me?

Not the promise.
Not the legacy.
Not the "main story."

Me.

Then a voice came—clear, direct, personal.

Not from the household I had fled.
Not from the people who had power over me.

From God.

He called me by name.

That sound—my name—was like water in a place with no water.

He didn't pretend my pain wasn't real.
He didn't excuse what had been done.
He didn't tell me to be grateful for my role in someone else's plan.

He spoke to me.

He saw me.

He gave me enough direction for the next step and enough promise for the road ahead.

I didn't know all the "why." I didn't get a full explanation for the mess. But I received something more stabilizing than explanation:

Presence.

And I said something that surprised even me, because it was the first time I had ever dared to name God from my own experience:

You are the God who sees me.

I wish I could tell you that everything got easy after that.

It didn't.

Years passed. The household changed again. The pressure shifted. And one day, I was sent away—again—this time with my son.

A child I loved.
A child the world labeled before he could speak.
A child born into a story he didn't ask for.

We walked until the water was gone.

When the last drops disappeared, fear turned into something heavier than fear—despair.

I laid my boy down under a bush and turned my face away because I could not bear to watch him die.

This is what the valley can do.
It can make you think: this is the end.
It can make you believe: God has forgotten.
It can make you feel: I am alone in the world.

But again, God moved toward me.

God heard.

Not only the prayers I could form—God heard the cries I couldn't translate into words. God heard the voice of a child in the wilderness. God heard the sound of a mother breaking.

And God provided.

He opened my eyes to what I could not see: water, provision, a next step.

Not a full map.
A next step.

And that is often how God leads people through the valley of the unknown.

He does not always give the full picture.
He gives enough for today.

He does not always erase the consequences.
He provides inside them.

He does not always undo the choices that harmed us.
He refuses to abandon us in the aftermath.

If your life has been affected by someone else's decision—if you have been the collateral damage of another person's fear—hear this:

God sees you.

If you are living with regret because your choices hurt someone you love—hear this too:

God's compassion reaches to everyone in the story.

He is not limited to the "main characters."
He does not only provide for the ones who feel righteous.
He shows up in the wilderness for the ones who feel discarded.

And He makes a way forward when you cannot see one.

The Gentle Truth

Sometimes the valley of the unknown isn't caused by something you chose. It's caused by something that happened to you—someone else's fear, someone else's impatience, someone else's decision.

God sees you in that place.

And even when the situation is complicated—when there is regret, harm, and collateral damage—God's compassion is not confused. He knows how to provide for everyone involved.

He may not give you the full map, but He will give you the next step.

A Small Practice for the Valley

If you feel unseen or displaced, pray this:

"God, I feel forgotten.
I feel pushed aside.
I feel like my story doesn't matter.
But if You see me, help me see You.
Give me the next step."

Then do one small act of care today:
- drink water and eat something simple,
- reach out to one safe person,
- take a two-minute pause to breathe,
- or write one sentence: "God sees me here."

Chapter Five

Empty Hands

**This chapter explores Naomi—
for anyone carrying loss that emptied your future, and needs courage to keep walking until provision appears.**

I left home full.

That's what makes the ending feel so cruel.

I had a husband. I had sons. I had plans. I had a name that meant something tender—pleasant, whole, blessed. I walked out with the kind of ordinary confidence you don't realize is a gift until it's gone.

Then the land dried up.

Food became scarce. Hunger has a way of shrinking the world until all you can think about is survival. So we did what families do when they're afraid—we moved. We crossed a border hoping the next place would be kinder than the last.

At first, it was supposed to be temporary.

Just until things improved.
Just until the famine passed.
Just until we could breathe again.

But valleys don't always announce how long they plan to stay.

Time moved forward, and life unraveled in slow, ordinary heartbreak.

One loss.
Then another.
Then the kind of loss that changes the air in the room.

My husband died.

It felt like a door slamming in the middle of the night—sudden, disorienting, final. I remember the silence afterward. The strange way the world keeps going even when yours stops.

My sons were still with me then. So I tried to keep going.

Because that's what women do in the valley: we keep going with shaking hands and tight throats. We cook. We clean. We plan. We pretend we can carry what we were never meant to carry alone.

But the valley wasn't finished.

My sons died too.

Both of them.

And something in me went numb. Not dramatic numb. Not the kind that looks like a movie. The kind that simply refuses to feel because feeling would crush you.

If you've ever sat in that kind of grief, you know what it does.

It makes the future feel like a closed gate.
It makes the past feel like a mocking photograph.
It makes God feel like a distant rumor.

People talk about God's faithfulness as if it's always warm. But sometimes, in the valley, faithfulness feels like a word other people can say but you can't taste anymore.

And then there was money.

Or rather—the lack of it.

Because grief is heavy, and poverty is heavy, and when they sit on your chest at the same time, it can feel like you can't breathe.

We were vulnerable—women without protection, without income, without a clear path. In my world, that wasn't just sad. It was dangerous.

And that's how the valley of the unknown can come: not as one single tragedy, but as a pile of them.

Loss on loss.
Bills with no answers.

Needs with no resources.
A future that feels like fog.

At some point, I stopped trying to polish it with hope.

I started speaking honestly.

I stopped using my old name.

Because "pleasant" no longer fit.

I told people to call me bitter.

Not because I wanted to be dramatic. Because bitterness felt like the only truthful language left.

And the worst part is, I thought I was protecting myself by saying it out loud—like if I named the ache, it would hurt less.

But naming the ache didn't make it smaller.

It just made the silence louder.

That's what bitterness does. It feels like honesty, but it can also become a wall. A wall you build to keep more pain out—only to realize later you've also kept comfort out.

So I decided to go home.

Not because I was hopeful.

Because I was tired.

I had heard there was bread again in the place I came from. And bread felt like a mercy I could understand. Not a miracle. Just food.

As I prepared to leave, I tried to release the women who had attached their lives to mine. I told them to go back. To start over. To find safety. To find husbands. To find a future I couldn't give them.

And one of them did.

But the other… she stayed.

Her loyalty made no sense to me.

She clung to me as if my broken life was still worth sharing. As if my empty hands could still hold something good. As if my God—who felt silent to me—was still worth trusting.

She spoke like love was stronger than loss.

And I didn't have the strength to argue.

So we walked together.

Two women.
Two widows.
Two sets of grief.
One uncertain road.

And when we arrived, I felt exposed.

Because home has a way of reminding you what you've lost.

People looked at me as if they were trying to recognize the version of me that left. I could see the questions in their eyes:

Is that really her?
What happened?
Where is your family?

And I said it again—the only language I trusted:

"Don't call me pleasant. Call me bitter."

It was my way of saying: don't expect me to sparkle. Don't ask me to pretend. Don't make me explain why life turned out like this.

But something was happening that I couldn't see yet.

God was not finished with my story.

Not because I finally believed hard enough.
Not because I cleaned up my bitterness.
Not because I said the right words.

But because God is the kind of God who can work with empty hands.

Provision didn't fall from the sky with a trumpet.

It came quietly—through fields and gleaning and ordinary kindness. Through a man who noticed.

Through lawful generosity. Through people doing the right thing in a hard world.

It came through community.
Through daily bread.
Through small mercies stacked one on top of another.

And slowly, the fog began to lift—not all at once, but enough to see the next step.

That's what God often does in the valley of the unknown.

He doesn't always change everything overnight.
He gives you enough for today.

He feeds you before He explains.
He provides before He resolves.
He restores in ways you may not recognize at first.

And sometimes—this is the hardest grace to receive—He uses someone else's faith to carry you when yours feels thin.

I didn't realize my story would become a story about redemption.

I thought it would remain a story about loss.

But God has a way of weaving new beginnings into the places we thought were finished.

Even for bitter women.
Even for empty hands.
Even for those who cannot see Him yet.

The Gentle Truth

Some valleys are made of practical burdens: grief, bills, scarcity, and uncertainty that won't let up. In those seasons, faith can feel quiet—not because God is gone, but because your heart is exhausted.

God is not offended by your honesty. He can handle your "bitter."

And when you have nothing left to give, God is still able to provide—often through ordinary means: daily bread, safe people, small mercies, and next steps.

Empty hands do not disqualify you. They make room for receiving.

A Small Practice for the Valley

If you feel overwhelmed by lack—financial, emotional, or relational—try this:

1) Name the need without shame (one sentence):
"God, I need ________."

2) Ask for today's provision (not the whole future): "Give me daily bread—one next step, one safe person, one workable plan."

3) Choose one practical step you can do today:
- make one phone call,
- open one bill and write one plan,
- ask someone trustworthy for help,
- apply for one resource,
- or rest for one hour without guilt.

If you can, whisper this as you do it: "God, I can't see You clearly, but I am still walking."

Chapter Six

When the Answers Don't Come

This chapter explores Job—
for anyone suffering without answers, and needs God's presence when explanations don't come.

I did not lose everything all at once.

That's what people assume—one thunderclap, one sweeping disaster, one headline that explains the collapse.

But loss came in waves.

The first messenger arrived out of breath, dust on his face, panic in his eyes. Before he even spoke, my body knew something had shifted. There is a kind of fear that moves through a room before the words arrive.

Then the words arrived.

Gone.
Stolen.
Destroyed.

Before I could stand up, another runner appeared. Then another. Then another—each one carrying news that sounded impossible, each one stacking grief on top of grief until it felt like the air itself was heavy.

By the time the final message came, I wasn't thinking like a man anymore. I was thinking like someone drowning—grabbing for anything that might keep me afloat.

And then I heard it.

My children.

All gone.

There are losses that hurt, and then there are losses that rearrange your soul. I remember reaching for the ground because standing felt dishonest—like my legs were pretending stability my heart no longer had.

People say you "go numb" in moments like that. That phrase is too gentle. It's not numbness. It's shock. It's the mind refusing to accept what the ears just heard. It's the body staying alive while something inside you falls silent.

I tore my clothes. Not for drama. Because grief has its own language, and my body needed to speak it.

I sat down because I could not imagine what to do next.

Everything I had built was gone.

My work.
My security.

My future.
My children.

And the first question that rose in my throat was not philosophical.

It was personal.

Where are You?

Not in the way people ask when they never believed. In the way believers ask when something sacred has been taken.

I had lived carefully.

That part matters too.

I had ordered my life around reverence and responsibility. I wasn't careless with people. I wasn't cruel. I wasn't indifferent. I tried to do what was right when no one was watching.

So when the collapse came, I wasn't only grieving—I was confused.

Because suffering feels different when you can't connect it to a reason.

At first, I tried to hold myself steady with what I knew.

God is good.
God is faithful.
God is wise.

But then the silence stretched long, and those sentences began to feel like words I had borrowed from other people's mouths—truths I still believed but couldn't feel in my bones.

And then my body began to fail too.

Pain is humbling. Pain takes the wide world and shrinks it down to skin and breath. Sores formed. My sleep broke into pieces. My thoughts spun in circles. I scraped my skin just to distract myself from what was happening inside me.

There is a particular loneliness when your body becomes another battlefield.

And then, as if grief needed witnesses, people came.

They sat with me at first—quiet, stunned, respectful. I was grateful for their silence. Silence can be mercy when words would wound.

But eventually, the quiet made them uncomfortable.

Because humans crave explanations. We want suffering to make sense. We want pain to fit into a box we can label and control.

So they began to explain.

They searched for causes. For mistakes I must have made. For hidden choices, secret compromises, private moments when I drifted from God's leading.

They asked questions like they were building a case.

Because randomness terrifies people.

It is easier to believe pain is earned than to accept that suffering can be unexplained.

Their explanations landed heavier than my grief.

Because when you are already shattered, being blamed feels unbearable.

I listened at first, trying to see if they were right—turning my life over in my mind like a stone, searching for cracks.

But the more they spoke, the more I realized they weren't trying to help me—they were trying to protect themselves.

If my suffering was my fault, then their lives were safe.
If the valley came because of a mistake, then they could avoid it.
If pain followed a formula, then God could be managed.

But God is not managed.

And grief is not solved.

So I said what I could not keep swallowing: I don't know why this is happening.

I wanted God.

Not shallow answers.
Not religious math.
Not platitudes shaped like wisdom.

I wanted Him to speak.
To clarify.
To explain.
To tell me what I was missing.

But heaven was quiet.

And that silence felt cruel.

If you've ever been there—crying out, searching, praying, begging—and hearing nothing back, you know how disorienting it is.

Silence makes you question not only God's presence, but your own worth.

It whispers: Maybe you weren't loved as much as you thought.
Maybe you misunderstood God.
Maybe you are alone.

And in that valley, you can do one of two things: you can pretend you're fine, or you can tell the truth.

I told the truth.

I said things I never thought I would say.

I asked questions that scared me.

I didn't wrap them in polite language. I didn't hide my disappointment. I didn't pretend I was strong.

And here's what surprised me most:

God did not strike me down for my honesty.

He did not pull away because I was angry.
He did not abandon me because I was confused.
He did not reject me because my faith had cracks.

When He finally spoke, it wasn't the explanation I wanted.

He didn't give me a timeline.
He didn't hand me a neat list of reasons.
He didn't justify the pain.
He didn't tell me how to avoid it next time.

Instead, He reminded me who He was.

Not distant.
Not careless.
Not small.

He spoke like thunder and tenderness braided together—like a Father who is not offended by your tears, but is also not reduced by your questions.

He showed me how vast He is.
How present He is.
How attentive He is—even when I couldn't see it.

And in that moment, I realized something I couldn't have learned any other way:

Faith is not always about understanding.
Sometimes it is about standing in the mystery and discovering you are not alone in it.

My circumstances did not immediately change.

The ache was still there.
The empty places were still empty.
The memories still hurt.

But something else changed.

I was no longer alone with my questions.

And that—strangely—was enough to take the next breath.

Because when God feels silent, it does not mean He is absent.

Sometimes it means He is deeper than our explanations.

And sometimes, in time, He restores—quietly, steadily—more than we imagined.

But even before restoration, His presence is a kind of resurrection.

The Gentle Truth

Some valleys arrive without warning and without explanation. They dismantle what felt stable and leave us searching for reasons that never come.

God is not offended by your questions. He is not threatened by your confusion. And He is not absent because He is silent.

You may not receive the answers you want—but you can receive His presence. And sometimes, that presence is what sustains you when clarity does not.

A Small Practice for the Valley

If God feels silent right now, try this:

Sit quietly for two minutes.
Place one hand on your chest.
Breathe slowly and say:

"God, I don't understand.
But I am still here.
Be with me in the not knowing."

If you want a Scripture to hold without forcing it, whisper this: "God is near to the brokenhearted." (Psalm 34:18)

You are not required to solve the mystery today. You are only invited to remain.

Chapter Seven

After the Win

This chapter explores Elijah—
for anyone who crashed after carrying too much,
and needs the holy rhythm of rest and gentle care.

I thought the hardest part would be the fight.

I was wrong.

The fight at least made sense.

There was a clear enemy, a clear line in the sand, a clear moment where you either stand or you fold. Adrenaline can carry you through those kinds of days. Purpose can make you brave. Even fear can be useful when it sharpens you into motion.

But there is a strange kind of danger that comes after the victory—after the shouting fades, after the crowd disperses, after the last "Amen" is spoken and you are finally alone with your own body again.

That's when the crash can come.

It starts quietly.

A tremor in your hands when no one is watching.
A heaviness behind your eyes.
A silence inside you that feels too wide.

People assume that if you've done something brave—if you've stood in faith—if you've watched God move in a way that makes people stare—you should feel untouchable afterward.

But I didn't.

I felt emptied out.

Like I had poured everything I had onto the altar, and now there was nothing left inside me to keep the fire going.

I had just seen God answer.

I had just watched impossible become visible.

I had just stood in the kind of moment people would remember for generations.

And yet one message—one threat—was enough to unravel me.

It's embarrassing to admit.

But the body doesn't care what you accomplished yesterday. The nervous system doesn't measure yesterday's miracle when it is flooded today. It only knows: danger. It only knows: run.

So I ran.

Not in a heroic way.
Not in a strategic way.
In a desperate way.

I moved like someone chased by something larger than circumstances. I moved like fear had become a voice in my bones, repeating the same sentence over and over:

Get away.
Get away.
Get away.

The road stretched long under my feet. My breath came in harsh bursts. My mind replayed every possible ending. Even the sky felt sharp.

And somewhere along the way, I realized I wasn't only running from the threat outside of me.

I was running from the crash inside of me.

From the sudden drop.
From the emptiness.
From the overwhelming realization that I could not keep holding everyone else's faith like it was my job.

I had done so much for so long that I didn't know how to stop.

And when you don't know how to stop, your body will eventually stop you.

I ended up alone under a tree.

A small shelter in a wide wilderness.

The sun was relentless. The air was hot. The silence was thick. And for the first time in a long time, I said the sentence I had been trying not to say:

I've had enough.

I didn't dress it up.
I didn't polish it into a holy phrase.
I didn't add a "but I trust You" at the end to make it sound better.

I've had enough.

That's the valley of the unknown, isn't it? The place where you don't know how to keep going. The place where the future feels like fog. The place where your faith feels thin and your strength feels gone.

Maybe your version isn't a wilderness under a tree.

Maybe yours is your kitchen at midnight.
A parking lot after work.
A hospital hallway.
A quiet bedroom where you stare at the ceiling and can't make your body move.

But the feeling is the same:

I can't do this anymore.

And what makes it worse is that you may have been doing "good" things. You may have been serving. Carrying. Showing up. Being strong for everyone else. Holding it together. Doing what needed to be done.

And then one more thing happens—and you crumble.

The crash is confusing because it comes after the win.

After the job promotion you worked so hard for.
After the season of ministry that demanded everything.
After the family crisis you held together.
After the months of pushing through.

You expected relief.

Instead you got collapse.

And in that collapse, God can feel far away—not because you stopped believing, but because you're too tired to feel anything at all.

I expected God to correct me.

To remind me of my calling.
To tell me to be brave.
To put me back on the road with a stern word and a holy push.

But that's not what happened.

God's first response to me was not a sermon.

It was rest.

I slept.

And when I woke up, there was food.

Bread.
Water.
A quiet kind of care that didn't demand anything from me.

I ate like someone who had forgotten what it felt like to be tended to.

Then I slept again.

And again, there was food.

Not a lecture.
Not a list of everything I should have done differently.
Not a spiritual performance review.

Just provision.

As if God knew what I was too exhausted to name: I didn't need more pressure. I needed my body to come back online.

Sometimes what we call a "spiritual crisis" is also a physical depletion.

Sometimes the loudest voice in the valley is not rebellion—it is exhaustion.

And God knows the difference.

He knows when your soul is weary and your nervous system is flooded. He knows when your tears are not a lack of faith but a lack of fuel.

He built you to need rest.

Not as a reward for finishing, but as part of being human.

Rest is not earned by finishing; rest is received because you are human.

After I ate and drank and slept, God led me deeper—away from the noise, away from the expectations, away from the crowd.

Into a place where I could finally hear again.

I thought God would meet me in the storm.

But when the storm came—wind ripping through the rocks, earth shaking under my feet, fire flashing in the darkness—I realized something:

God was not in the chaos.

And then, after the noise, there was a sound so small I almost missed it.

A gentle whisper.
A quiet presence.
A steadiness that didn't shout.

That's how God comes sometimes in the valley—when you can't handle volume. When your system is overwhelmed. When your heart is bruised.

He doesn't always come louder.

He often comes nearer.

And in that quiet, God did something else I didn't expect.

He gave me perspective.

He reminded me I wasn't alone.
That I wasn't the only one still faithful.
That my life was bigger than the fear in my chest.
That the story wasn't ending with me under a tree.

He didn't minimize the threat.
He didn't pretend the pressure wasn't real.

But He refused to let my exhaustion write the ending.

That's what fear does—it tries to narrate your future while you are depleted.

But depletion is a terrible narrator.

When you are exhausted, everything feels permanent.
When you are depleted, everything feels hopeless.

When you are burned out, every door looks like it's closing.

So God gave me a rhythm: rest, nourishment, quiet, then direction.

Not direction first.

Rest first.

If you are in the valley after the win—if you are crashing after carrying too much—hear this gently:

Your crash does not mean you are weak.
It means you are human.

God is not disappointed in your need for rest.
He designed you with limits.
He meets you in them.

And when you cannot see Him, start with the simplest faithfulness you can manage:

Sleep.
Eat.
Breathe.
Ask for help.
Return to quiet.

God can speak in a whisper.
And His whisper is enough to lead you one step at a time.

He did not abandon me in the crash.

He fed me.
He let me sleep.
He met me in the quiet.
And He sent me back into life with mercy—not shame.

That is what the God you cannot see is doing even now: putting His hand in yours, restoring your strength, and guiding you through the fog.

The Gentle Truth

Some valleys come right after a season of intense output—after you've carried pressure, responsibility, or spiritual weight for longer than your body can sustain.

A crash after a win is not proof that you failed. It is often proof that you are depleted.

God's first response is often care: rest, nourishment, and quiet. He does not shame you back into strength. He restores you.

A Small Practice for the Valley

If you feel burned out or on the edge of a crash, try this "rest rhythm check":

1) Body: Have I slept? eaten? hydrated?
2) Load: What am I carrying that isn't mine to carry alone?
3) Quiet: Where can I find ten minutes of calm today?

Prayer (keep it simple):

"God, my body is tired.
My mind is loud.
Meet me with rest.
Speak to me in the quiet.
Show me one next step."

If movement is helpful and accessible today, take a short walk (if that's accessible today) and breathe slowly for five minutes.

Chapter Eight

The Pit and the Fog

This chapter explores Joseph—
for anyone betrayed and misunderstood,
and needs to know God can redeem what others meant for harm.

I used to think the dream meant the path would be clear.

I thought if God showed you something, it would come with a map.

But the first place I learned about calling was not on a stage or in a spotlight.

It was at the bottom of a pit.

It happened fast.

One day I was walking toward my brothers with food in my hands and the sun on my shoulders. The next, I was falling—arms flailing, breath catching, dirt scraping my skin as I hit the ground hard.

Above me, their faces were silhouettes against the sky.

I could hear them talking.

Laughing.

Deciding what to do with me like I was a problem to solve instead of a person to love.

I called out. I pleaded. I tried to reason.

But when people are committed to misunderstanding you, your words don't land. They bounce off their assumptions and fall back down into the hole with you.

That's one of the hardest valleys of the unknown: when you don't just lose your footing—you lose your place.

You lose the sense that you belong.
You lose the sense that you are safe.
You lose the sense that your life is still your own.

From the pit, everything looked different.

The sky felt farther away.
Time moved slower.
Hope felt like something that belonged to other people.

And I kept thinking the same thought, again and again:

God… where are You?

Because I had not asked for this.

I had not chosen betrayal.
I had not chosen jealousy.
I had not chosen to be the target of someone else's resentment.

I had simply been… me.

And somehow that was enough to make them hate me.

They pulled me out of the pit eventually—but not to restore me.

To sell me.

I remember the grip on my arms. The rope. The rough hands. The feeling of being traded like livestock. The shock of realizing my life had been reduced to a price.

And as the caravan moved away, I watched the hills of my home disappear until the horizon swallowed them.

There are departures you choose.
And then there are departures that feel like death.

This was the second kind.

New land. New language. New masters. New rules.

I learned quickly that survival in a foreign place requires a kind of vigilance you don't need at home.

You watch tone. You watch expression. You watch for danger before it announces itself.

And in the middle of that, I tried to stay faithful.

Not because I felt strong.

Because faithfulness was the only piece of myself I could still control.

I worked hard. I served well. I tried to live with integrity even when no one would have blamed me for giving up.

And for a moment, it looked like the fog might lift.

Responsibility came.
Trust came.
A kind of stability formed.

I thought: Maybe this is the chapter where God brings me back to the dream.

Then the next valley arrived.

Not from my work.
Not from my choices.
From someone else's story colliding with mine.

A lie can undo years of faithfulness in a single sentence.

I was accused of what I did not do.

And in a world where power decides truth, my innocence didn't matter.

I was thrown into prison—the kind of place that does not care about nuance. The kind of place that teaches you how little control you actually have.

Iron doors.
Stone walls.
Days that blur.
Nights that stretch.

This is what the valley of the unknown can feel like: doing your best and still getting crushed.

You start asking different questions.

Not "What did I do wrong?"
But "What does faith even mean if obedience doesn't protect me?"

And if you're honest, you begin to wonder:

Was the dream real?
Or did I imagine it?
Was God speaking?
Or was I simply hopeful?

Prison does that. So does long disappointment. So does waiting with no update.

Time is heavy when you cannot see what it is producing.

But something was happening in the dark that I could not see.

God was doing quiet work.

Not the kind that makes for quick testimonies.
The kind that builds endurance.
The kind that shapes character.
The kind that teaches you how to remain yourself in a place designed to erase you.

I learned how to listen in the dark.

To notice the small mercies.
To pay attention to the ways God shows up without announcements.

A conversation.
A moment of favor.
A door that cracks open just enough to let light in.

Then came the strangest thing: even in prison, I was given responsibility.

Which sounds like a blessing until you realize responsibility can also feel like delay wearing a disguise.

Because the longer you serve well, the easier it is for people to forget you belong somewhere else.

I helped someone once—interpreted a dream, offered hope, spoke truth when despair was thick. And for a moment, I thought, This is it. This is how God brings me out.

But then that person left.

And forgot me.

Not because they were cruel—because they were relieved. Because freedom makes people eager to move on from the places that smelled like suffering.

And I stayed behind.

More waiting.
More fog.
More days that felt the same.

If you've ever felt forgotten—truly forgotten—this part of the story will make sense to you.

Forgotten is not just loneliness.
It's a question mark.
It's the feeling that your life is paused while everyone else's is moving.

And in that place, God can feel invisible.

But invisibility is not absence.

Here is what I learned in the slow years:

God can be present even when you cannot trace Him.
God can be working even when you cannot measure it.

God can be faithful even when your circumstances look like rejection.

The pit did not mean the dream was dead.
The prison did not mean God had changed His mind.
The fog did not mean I had been abandoned.

It meant I was in process.

And in time—God's time, not mine—the doors opened.

Not because I forced them.
Not because I performed perfectly.
Not because I convinced anyone.

Because God has a way of lifting people out of pits without needing permission from the ones who pushed them in.

And when it finally happened, it happened quickly—almost like the blink of an eye after years of slow.

That is how God sometimes works in the valley.

Long quiet.
Then sudden shift.

But even before the shift, God's hand was on me.

Holding me steady in the fog.
Keeping my heart alive in the dark.
Teaching me to see Him without needing the sun.

The Gentle Truth

Some valleys are made of betrayal, false accusation, and long delays—seasons where your life feels derailed by someone else's choices.

When that happens, it's easy to assume God has forgotten you.

But a hidden season is not a wasted season. God can be present in the pit, faithful in the prison, and purposeful in the fog—even when you cannot see how the pieces fit.

A Small Practice for the Valley

If you feel stuck in a long, unclear season, try this:

1) Name what is true (one sentence):
"God, I feel forgotten."

2) Ask for today's mercy (not the whole future):
"Give me today's strength and one next step."

3) Choose one integrity action you can take today:
- do one small task with excellence,
- tell the truth kindly,
- refuse to retaliate,
- or reach out to one safe person for support.

Prayer:

"God, I can't see the map.
But I choose faithfulness in the fog.
Hold me steady until the next door opens."

Chapter Nine

The Long Walk Home

This chapter explores the prodigal son—for anyone who made a mess and wonders if home is still possible, and needs a Father whose mercy runs.

I practiced the speech until it sounded believable.

Not because I thought it would change anything—because I needed something to hold in my mouth besides fear.

"I am no longer worthy."
"Just let me work."
"I don't deserve to be called your child."

I repeated it like a rope in my hands.

Because I was walking toward a door I didn't know would open.

And that is what the valley of the unknown can feel like—moving forward without any guarantee of mercy. Taking steps while your stomach turns. Hoping for kindness while preparing for humiliation.

I had once imagined freedom as bright.

Leaving home had felt like oxygen.

I wanted my own life. My own choices. My own story. I was tired of boundaries and expectations and the quiet weight of someone else's authority. I wanted the world to be wide and my days to be mine.

So I asked for what I had not earned yet.

And my father gave it.

People don't understand that part.

They assume he should have stopped me. They assume love must control. They assume the right thing is to tighten the grip when someone is about to make a mistake.

But love—true love—sometimes lets you walk.

Not because it approves of the direction.
Because it refuses to remove your dignity.

He gave me what I demanded, and I left quickly—as if speed could prevent regret.

At first, it was everything I thought I wanted.

Money feels like power when you've never held it.
New friends feel like belonging when you've never tested loyalty.
New experiences feel like life when you're hungry for sensation.

And for a while, I felt invincible.

Until I didn't.

Because the world is generous at the beginning.

It gives you a taste. It gives you applause. It gives you the illusion that you are in control.

Then it takes payment.

I spent too quickly. Trusted too easily. Chased too hard. I tried to fill an emptiness I couldn't name with anything that sparkled.

And the moment the money ran out, so did the smiles.

That's what scarcity does—it reveals what is real.

When I had resources, people found me.
When I had nothing, I became invisible.

Then the famine came.

As if my personal collapse wasn't enough, the land itself dried up. Food became scarce. Work became scarce. Hope became scarce.

I took whatever job I could find.

And I ended up feeding animals I never imagined being near.

I had left home to feel important, and now my hands were covered in dirt and my stomach was aching with hunger. I watched the animals eat and realized I wanted their food.

That's when the fog thickened.

Not because I couldn't see my situation.
Because I could.

I could see how far I had fallen.

And what I couldn't see—what terrified me—was whether anyone would still want me after this.

Shame is a strange companion in the valley.

It doesn't always scream.
Sometimes it whispers steadily, like a drip you can't turn off:

You ruined this.
You're disgusting.
You don't deserve to go back.
You don't deserve to be loved.

I started to believe that my failure had changed my identity.
That what I had done was now who I was.

So I practiced the speech again.

Not because I wanted to be a servant.

Because I thought it was the only way to survive my own shame.

Then, one morning, something inside me shifted.

Not a miracle.

A memory.

I remembered bread.

I remembered warmth.
I remembered a table that didn't require me to earn my seat.
I remembered a father who didn't treat me like a transaction.

And for the first time in a long time, hope didn't feel like fantasy.

It felt like a direction.

So I started walking.

The road home felt longer than the road away. Every step was a conversation with my own regret.

What if he closes the door?
What if he lets me in but never looks me in the eyes again?
What if he only tolerates me?
What if I'm too late?

I kept rehearsing my unworthiness.

Because if I expected rejection, it wouldn't hurt as much.

But love has a way of surprising you when you least expect it.

I wasn't even close to the house when I saw him.

Running.

Not walking.
Not standing on the porch with arms crossed.
Running.

A man like him didn't run.
Dignity didn't run.

But he did.

And before my speech could leave my mouth, before I could explain myself or earn anything or bargain for a lesser position, his arms were around me.

I smelled the familiar scent of home and tears and sweat.
I felt his grip—firm, present, unmistakably real.

And I realized something in that moment:

The valley had convinced me I was disowned.

But I was still his son.

My shame had narrated a story God was not telling.

Because this is what shame does: it tries to write the ending while you're still walking.

It tells you God is done with you.
That you've gone too far.
That you've broken what cannot be repaired.

But God is not fragile.

And love is not afraid of your mess.

My father didn't ask for the speech.

He interrupted it.

He cut through my rehearsed unworthiness with celebration.

He called for a robe—the kind you wear when you belong.
A ring—the kind you wear when you have a name.
Sandals—the kind you wear when you are not a slave.

Then he did something that still stuns me:

He threw a feast.

Not because I had performed well.
Because I had returned.

I had assumed the goal was perfection.
He revealed the goal was relationship.

And that's what I want you to know if you are walking through a valley filled with regret:

God is not waiting to punish you when you come home.
He is watching for you.

Even now.

He is not measuring your speech.
He is moving toward your heart.

And if you can take one step—one honest step in His direction—mercy will meet you on the road.

Not as a reward for good behavior.

As a welcome.

Because you are still family.

The Gentle Truth

Regret can make the road back feel impossible. Shame convinces us that our worst choices have permanently changed our identity.

But God's love is not transactional. He is not waiting to hear a perfect speech before He offers mercy.

When you return—even with shaking hands—He meets you with welcome. The goal is not perfection. The goal is relationship.

A Small Practice for the Valley

If you're coming home after a hard season—spiritually, relationally, or emotionally—try this:

1) Tell the truth (one sentence):
"God, I'm afraid to come back."

2) Take one step of return today:
- pray one honest prayer,
- open your Bible to one Psalm,
- text one safe person,
- show up to one service,
- or schedule one conversation.

Prayer:

"Father, I don't have perfect words.
I only have my return.
Meet me on the road.
Remind me I am still Yours."

Chapter Ten

When the Numbers Don't Work

This chapter explores the widow—
for anyone staring at numbers that don't work,
and needs to see what God can do with what is
already in your hands.

The knock at the door sounded like judgment.

It wasn't loud, but it carried a weight that made my stomach tighten before I even moved. I knew what it meant. I knew who it would be. I knew the words that were coming, because I had heard them in my mind for days—maybe weeks—like a drumbeat in the dark.

Pay what you owe.

Debt does that. It lives in your thoughts. It follows you into sleep. It turns ordinary moments into dread.

I wasn't lazy. I wasn't careless. I wasn't trying to avoid responsibility.

I was overwhelmed.

My husband had died, and with him went more than companionship. He had been the structure of our home—the steady hands, the earning, the protection. When he was gone, the world didn't pause to let me catch my breath.

Grief arrived first.

Then reality came with receipts.

Bills.
Obligations.
Promises made before I ever had to carry them alone.

I tried to manage it quietly. I tried to stretch what we had. I sold what I could. I made meals smaller and prayers bigger. I did the math again and again, as if rechecking would change the outcome.

But the numbers didn't work.

And in the valley of the unknown, when the numbers don't work, fear gets loud.

Not the kind of fear that feels dramatic.

The kind that feels practical.

The kind that asks: What will happen to my children?

Because in my world, unpaid debt wasn't just embarrassing. It was dangerous. Debt could take more than your peace. It could take your future.

It could take your sons.

That's the part people don't always understand when they say, "Just trust God."

Trusting God doesn't erase the real consequences you're staring at. It doesn't make your stomach stop turning. It doesn't magically remove the pressure of a deadline.

It simply means you take your fear into the presence of Someone steadier than your fear.

But that day at the door, my fear felt bigger than my faith.

I opened it anyway.

The creditor's eyes were not cruel. They were simply certain—certain of the law, certain of what would happen next if I couldn't pay.

I pleaded.

I explained.

I tried to buy time with words I didn't have enough breath to say.

And when the door finally closed, I slid down the wall and pressed my forehead into my hands, because crying felt like the only honest thing left.

I could not see a way out.

And the worst part wasn't just the debt.

It was the feeling that I had failed my family.

Maybe you know that shame.

The shame of not being able to provide.
The shame of watching your children need things you can't give.
The shame of being the one adults look at with quiet pity.

When you're in debt to your eyeballs, it can feel like you're buried alive—still breathing, still working, still trying, but trapped under a weight you can't lift.

I wanted God to do something big.

A miracle that would erase the numbers and silence the knock at the door forever.

But when I finally went to the man of God, his first question wasn't what I expected.

What do you have?

I almost laughed—not because it was funny, but because it was absurd.

What do I have?

I had debt.
I had fear.
I had empty cupboards.
I had children with wide eyes.
I had grief.

What do I have?

I told him the truth.

Nothing… except a small jar.

It wasn't impressive. It wasn't enough. It wasn't even worth mentioning, except he asked.

And he looked at that "not enough" like it mattered.

Then he gave me instructions that sounded strange—almost too simple for a problem this heavy.

Go borrow empty jars.
Not a few.
Go into your house.
Shut the door.
Pour.

This is where the valley gets uncomfortable, because God's provision often asks us to participate.

He doesn't always drop answers from the sky.
He sometimes asks us to gather emptiness.

To bring what we have.
To obey with what we can.
To move in the direction of hope before we feel hopeful.

I wanted to argue.

I wanted to say: Sir, you do not understand the numbers.
You do not understand the deadline.
You do not understand the fear.

But desperation has a way of making you try what you wouldn't normally try.

So I did it.

I borrowed jars from neighbors—humbling, awkward, holy. Every knock on their doors felt like admitting I couldn't hold my life together by myself.

Some people were kind.
Some were curious.
Some looked away too quickly.

But I kept asking.

Empty jars piled up in my house like a question: What now?

Then I closed the door.

Just me and my sons and the small jar that wasn't enough.

And I began to pour.

At first, my hands shook. I poured like someone expecting disappointment—like someone bracing for the moment the last drop would fall and prove what I already feared.

But it didn't stop.

The oil kept coming.

Jar after jar.
Empty becoming full.
Not by my strength.
Not by my strategy.
By God's quiet abundance in a closed room.

My sons watched with their mouths open.
I watched with tears on my face.
The air felt different—like hope had entered without making a sound.

And then the oil stopped.

Not because God ran out.

Because there were no more empty jars.

That detail stayed with me.

Sometimes the limit isn't God's supply.
It's our capacity to receive.

And in that moment, I realized something I want you to know too:

God is not intimidated by your numbers.

He is not overwhelmed by your debt.
He is not confused by your bills.
He is not late to your deadline.

He can provide in ways that don't make sense on paper.

But He often begins with what you have—however small—and what you can do—however humble.

And then He fills the empty places.

I sold the oil.

I paid the debt.

My sons stayed with me.

And we lived—not just surviving, but breathing again.

If you are in a valley where the numbers don't work—if you are staring at bills, pressure, uncertainty, and you can't see the light of day—hear this:

God sees your need.
He knows what's at stake.
He is able to provide.

And sometimes the miracle looks like this:

One next step.
One open door.

One small jar.
One room where God meets you with enough.

The Gentle Truth

Financial pressure can make the valley feel relentless. When the numbers don't work, fear becomes practical—and shame often follows.

But God is not intimidated by what overwhelms you. He can provide through surprising means, and He often begins with what is already in your hand.

He does not ask you to pretend the pressure isn't real. He invites you to bring your real need into His presence—and take the next step He gives you.

A Small Practice for the Valley

If you're under financial strain, try this gentle two-part practice:

1) Prayer of honesty:
"God, the numbers don't work.
I feel afraid and ashamed.
Show me what I have.
Show me the next step.
Provide what I cannot create."

2) One practical next step (choose one today):

- list your debts and deadlines on paper,
- call a creditor and ask for a payment plan,
- ask a trusted person for guidance,
- seek a community resource,
- or make one small budget decision.

Then whisper: "God, fill the empty places."

Chapter Eleven

When Your Heart Won't Sing

This chapter explores David—
for anyone who feels spiritually numb and can't make your heart sing, and needs permission to be honest while God holds you steady.

I have written songs for other people's storms.

That is the strange thing.

I have sung about God's goodness when the sun was shining and when it wasn't. I have put words to worship so others could borrow them when their own words ran out.

So when the silence came, I assumed I could out-sing it.

I assumed I could pray it away.
Work it away.
Write it away.

But this kind of valley doesn't leave because you try harder.

It arrives like fog—quiet, thick, slow—and one day you realize you haven't felt God's nearness in a long time.

Not in a dramatic way.
In a dull way.

The kind of dull that scares you because it feels like something holy has gone missing.

I kept showing up.

That's what faithful people do.
We keep showing up.

I went through the motions.
I spoke the right words.
I led the prayer.
I read the Scripture.

And inside, I felt… nothing.

Not anger.
Not passion.
Not even tears.

Just a numbness that made everything sound far away—including God.

If you've ever experienced spiritual numbness, you know how unsettling it is.

Because it doesn't feel like you're rebelling.
It feels like you're disappearing.

You start questioning things you never questioned before.

Am I broken?
Have I offended God?
Did He leave?
Did I?
Is this what it looks like when faith dies quietly?

People around you don't always notice. Numbness is easy to hide. You can smile. You can serve. You can laugh at the right moments. You can still do all the "Christian things" and feel like a stranger inside your own worship.

And the shame that follows is subtle.

Because you tell yourself: If anyone should feel God, it should be me.

I've seen too much.
I've received too much.
I've been rescued too many times.

So why can't I feel Him now?

The valley can do that—make you measure your faith by your emotions.

But emotions are not the same as presence.

And presence is not always loud.

Sometimes it is simply there, holding you, while you can't sense it.

I tried to fix myself.

I changed routines.
I added disciplines.
I cut out distractions.
I worked harder.

But the harder I pushed, the more exhausted I became.

And exhaustion makes numbness worse.

One night, I couldn't keep pretending.

So I told the truth.

Not in polished prayer language.
Not in worship words.

Just the truth.

How long?

How long will You feel distant?
How long will my prayers hit the ceiling and fall back down?
How long will I walk with a heart that can't sing?

That is the kind of prayer people don't like to quote on inspirational posters.

But it is Scripture.

It is holy honesty.

Because God included prayers like that in His Word to give permission to people like us—people who love Him and still feel lost in the fog.

I learned to pray with borrowed words.

Not to hide—because I couldn't create new ones.

I prayed the ancient prayers that sound like my own heart when it is tired.

I learned to say: "God, I trust You," even when I didn't feel it.

I learned to whisper: "God, don't forget me," even when I was ashamed to ask.

And over time—slowly, quietly—the numbness began to shift.

Not because the valley disappeared overnight.

But because I stopped measuring God's presence by my sensations and started measuring it by His character.

He is steady.
He is faithful.
He is near to the brokenhearted.
He does not despise a bruised reed.
He does not abandon the trembling.

I began to notice the small kindnesses again.

A friend's voice.
A sunrise.
A moment of laughter that felt real.
A Scripture that didn't feel like a task but like a hand on my shoulder.

Sometimes the valley doesn't end with fireworks.

Sometimes it ends with feeling again.

With a single tear.
With a deep breath.
With the quiet return of desire.

And even if you are not there yet, hear this:

Numbness is not the same as absence.

The fog is not the same as abandonment.

And your inability to "feel" God is not proof that God is far away.

It may simply be proof that you are tired.

So let your faith be small today.

Small faith still holds.

Borrow a Psalm.
Borrow a prayer.
Borrow a sentence.

God is not waiting for your heart to sing before He stays near.

He is near first.

And in time, your heart will sing again.

The Gentle Truth

Spiritual numbness can feel frightening because it looks like distance, but it often comes from fatigue, grief, or prolonged stress.

God's presence is not measured by your emotions. You can't feel Him and still be held by Him.

When your heart won't sing, borrow the prayers God has already given you. That is not fake faith—it is faithful endurance.

A Small Practice for the Valley

If you feel spiritually numb, try this gentle "borrowed prayer" practice:

1) Choose one Psalm to borrow today (Psalm 13, 42, or 23).
2) Read it slowly out loud.
3) Circle (or write down) one line that sounds like you.
4) Turn that line into your prayer.

Simple prayer:

"God, I can't feel You.
But I am still reaching.
Hold me in the fog.
Teach my heart to sing again."

Chapter Twelve

When I Crossed the Line

This chapter explores David—
for anyone who crossed a line and carries regret, and needs grace that restores without denying truth.

I did not wake up that morning planning to ruin my life.

That is what people don't understand about moral collapse.

It rarely begins with a dramatic decision.
It begins with small permissions.

A moment of entitlement.
A moment of unchecked desire.
A moment where you tell yourself, I deserve this.

It was a season where power had become normal to me.

The battles had been fought. The victories had stacked up. People spoke my name with admiration. My word carried weight. My presence turned heads. I had become the kind of man who could decide things and watch the world rearrange itself around my decisions.

That is a dangerous place for the human heart.

Because when no one challenges you, you start believing you are above the rules that keep everyone else safe.

And on a night that should have been ordinary, I looked too long.

I lingered where I should have turned away.

And something in me whispered a lie so smooth it sounded like truth:

No one will know.

But the lie beneath that lie was worse:

It won't matter.

I wish I could tell you the moment I crossed the line felt like fireworks.

It didn't.

It felt quiet.
It felt easy.
It felt like I was taking something I wanted.

And then it was done.

For a moment, I tried to move on as if it was only a private failure.

But a drift from God's leading rarely stays private.

It travels.
It touches other lives.
It multiplies.

And when the message came, fear grabbed me by the throat.

Not the fear of God.
The fear of exposure.

I began doing what people do when they're desperate to protect an image.

I controlled.
I manipulated.
I used power to manage consequences.

And every attempt to cover the mess only made it worse.

Because when you are trying to hide what you've done, you stop asking, What is right?
You start asking, What will keep me safe?

I crossed another line.
Then another.

Until I was buried under my own choices.

God sent someone to me.

Not with a sword.
With a story.

And when I finished condemning the man in the story, the voice said quietly:

You are the man.

I expected God to crush me.

He confronted me.
He named it.
He exposed it.

And then He offered a way back.

Not without consequences.
Not without truth.

But with mercy.

I didn't write a polished apology.

I wrote a prayer with shaking hands.

Have mercy.

Healing began when I stopped hiding.

God did not excuse my actions.
But He did not abandon me.

Repentance reopened the relationship.

And that is what I want you to know:

God sees your worst.
And He stays.

You may face consequences.
But you are not disqualified.

The valley does not have to be the end.

It can be the place where truth restores you.

The Gentle Truth

God's mercy does not deny harm—it brings it into the light so healing can begin. Repentance is not self-hatred. It is the courage to stop hiding and return.

A Small Practice for the Valley

Name the truth. Own the impact. Ask for a clean heart. Take one step toward repair.

Prayer:
God, I crossed lines.
I don't want to hide anymore.
Give me a clean heart.
Show me the next right step.

Chapter Thirteen

The Shepherd Who Kept Me

This chapter explores David—
for anyone who wonders if your victories are canceled by your valleys, and needs to live forward as a beloved child of God.

They remember the giant.

That part follows you.

Even now, when people speak my name, I can see the scene in their eyes—the boy, the sling, the stone, the impossible falling like it was always going to fall.

They don't remember the days before it.

They don't remember the long afternoons in open fields, watching sheep and watching skies, learning what it means to stay alert when no one is applauding. They don't remember the nights I slept light because predators don't announce themselves. They don't remember the small, steady faith of ordinary responsibility.

But that is where my courage was formed.

In the quiet.
In the unseen.
In the repetition.

Before the giant, there was a lion.

A sudden rush.
A flash of teeth.
The sound of terror in the flock.

My hands moved before my thoughts could fully catch up. I remember the weight of fear in my chest—and something deeper than fear underneath it: a steadiness I could not explain.

I was not brave because I was fearless.

I was brave because I believed I was not alone.

Before the giant, there was a bear.

Another moment where strength was demanded from a boy who had no reason to think he could handle it. Another moment where my life felt too small for the battle in front of me—and yet I stepped forward anyway.

That is what faith often looks like:

Not the absence of danger.
The presence of God.

Then came the day everyone tells.

The day the field turned into a stage.

There was shouting and armor and men who looked ready but weren't. There was fear dressed up as strategy. And there was a giant whose voice sounded like certainty.

I walked toward him with a sling and smooth stones in my pouch.

Not because I believed in myself.

Because I had learned—again and again—what God can do when you have only enough faith for the next step.

I don't remember the exact moment the stone left my hand. I remember the stillness afterward—the stunned silence, the sudden release in the crowd, the realization that the impossible can fall.

And I remember this too:

Victory didn't make God closer.

God was already close.

People assume the victories are where faith lives.

But faith also lives in caves.

That was my next classroom.

Because after the celebration came the chase. After the songs came the suspicion. After I proved myself came the season where I was hunted like an animal.

I learned what it feels like to live with a knot in your stomach—never sure where the next threat would come from, never sure if the people you trusted would be safe to trust tomorrow.

I learned what it feels like to sleep with one eye open and pray with the other.

I learned what it means to do the right thing and still be misunderstood.

And I learned something else in those caves:

God's faithfulness does not depend on my comfort.

He was with me when crowds cheered.
He was with me when caves echoed.
He was with me when my own heart was tired of being brave.

Then there were battles.

So many battles.

Some I won with clear strength. Some I survived by mercy alone. Some were fought in daylight with soldiers at my side. Some were fought in midnight silence with my thoughts as the enemy.

I watched God give me victories I couldn't have orchestrated.

I also watched Him lead me slowly—teaching me patience, teaching me humility, teaching me what it means to wait even when I wanted to act.

There were moments I worshiped without effort.

Moments when the presence of God felt like air—everywhere, undeniable, sustaining.

And then there were moments when I could not feel Him at all.

That part surprises people.

Because they imagine a straight line from giant-slaying to unshakable faith.

But spiritual life is not always a straight line.

It is a braid.

Courage and fear.
Worship and silence.
Victory and waiting.
Strength and trembling.

I have been all of those things.

And here is the truth I want you to hear in your own valley:

Your story is not canceled by your hardest season.

Not even if you have been numb.
Not even if you have failed.
Not even if you have regrets you would do anything to erase.

God's presence is not only for the highlight reel.

He is also the Shepherd in the shadowed places.

He kept me in the fields.
He kept me in the battle.
He kept me in the cave.
He kept me when I could not keep myself.

That is what makes faith possible after the fog.

Not my consistency.

His.

So when people call me "a man after God's own heart," I don't hear a compliment about perfection.

I hear a story about returning.

Because I have returned—again and again.

Returned from fear.
Returned from wandering thoughts.
Returned from numbness.
Returned from shame.
Returned from self-defense.
Returned into mercy.

And every time I returned, I found Him there—steady, present, not startled by the mess of being human.

If you are trying to live forward—trying to blaze a future with God's intended plan while carrying a past that still aches—remember this:

God can lead you in the present without pretending the past didn't happen.

He can restore your soul without rewriting history.

He can use you—not because you are flawless, but because He is faithful.

And if you will keep returning—one honest step at a time—you will discover what I discovered:

The Shepherd keeps you.

He restores you.

He leads you.

Even when you can't see Him.

The Gentle Truth

God's love is not limited to your best season. He is the Shepherd in your victories and in your valleys. A heart after God's heart is not a flawless heart—it is a returning heart.

A Small Practice for the Valley

Try this "returning" practice for the next seven days:

1) Morning: "God, I return to You today."
2) Midday (one breath): "Keep me close."
3) Night: "Where did I drift? Where did I return?"

Write one line each night. Not to perform—just to notice the rhythm.

Chapter Fourteen

When I Couldn't Believe Without Proof

**This chapter explores Thomas—
for anyone who can't believe without proof right now, and needs Jesus to meet you with peace, not shame.**

They told me He was alive.

And I wanted to believe them.

That's what made it so painful.

If the news had come from strangers, I could have dismissed it. If it had come from people who didn't know the weight of loss, I could have nodded politely and walked away.

But it came from my friends—the ones who had walked the same roads I walked, slept under the same skies, watched the same hands heal and the same mouth speak truth that made your heart feel clean.

They said, "We have seen Him."

I stared at them like they were speaking a language I couldn't understand.

Because I had seen something too.

I had seen Him arrested.
I had seen the fear.
I had seen the blood.
I had seen the finality in the eyes of people who were determined to end Him.

And I had seen what death does.

Death doesn't feel like a plot twist when you're standing near it.
It feels like a wall.

So when my friends said, "He's alive," something inside me tightened—hope and dread tangled together in the same breath.

Hope whispered: Please.
Dread answered: Don't.

Because hope can be cruel when you've been shattered.

Hope can feel like setting yourself up to break twice.

I wanted to protect what was left of my heart.

So I said what I needed to say to survive the moment:

Unless I see it… unless I touch it… I will not believe.

People have used my words against me for a long time.

They call it doubt like it's rebellion.

But doubt isn't always defiance.

Sometimes doubt is grief trying to keep you safe.

Sometimes it's the nervous system saying, "I can't take another loss."
Sometimes it's the mind saying, "I need something solid."
Sometimes it's the heart saying, "I want to trust, but I don't know how."

If you've ever lived through something that cracked your sense of safety—loss, betrayal, trauma, sickness, collapse—then you know why faith can suddenly feel harder.

Not because God changed.

Because you did.

Your body remembers.
Your mind replays.
Your spirit hesitates.

And you can love God and still say, "I need proof."

I spent eight days in that place.

Eight days is not long on a calendar.
But it can be an eternity when you're waiting for God to show up.

The others were glowing with their stories.

They talked about peace and forgiveness and presence. They used words like "joy" and "hope" as if those things were simple again.

And I was happy for them.

I really was.

But I also felt alone.

Because their certainty made my uncertainty feel like failure.

Have you ever been there?

Watching other people say, "God is so near," while you are silently thinking, "Why can't I feel Him?"

Hearing testimonies that sound like sunshine while you are living under clouds.

It's a strange kind of loneliness—being surrounded by faith and still feeling like you're outside the room.

I tried to pray.

But my prayers sounded thin.

Not angry. Just tired.

"God… if You're there… help me."

I tried to remember what I knew.

I tried to replay the miracles, the teachings, the way my heart burned when He spoke.

But memory can only carry you so far when you are in a present that hurts.

And that is the valley of the unknown:
when what you know is true and what you feel is empty.

I didn't want to become bitter.

I didn't want to become cynical.

But I also couldn't pretend.

So I stayed honest.

I stayed with my friends, even when I felt different from them.
I stayed near the story, even when I couldn't feel it.
I stayed within reach, even when I was not sure He would reach back.

And then—He came.

Not with anger.
Not with scolding.
Not with the tone of someone disappointed in my weakness.

He came with peace.

And the first thing He did was speak my language.

He didn't force me to speak His.
He stepped into mine.

He looked at me and said, in effect:

You want proof? Here.

Put your hands where you said you needed to put them.
Touch what you said you needed to touch.
See what you said you needed to see.

He met my trembling faith with gentleness.

He didn't call me foolish for needing reassurance.
He didn't shame me for being cautious.
He didn't compare me to everyone else in the room.

He simply showed up.

That's what changed me.

Not the argument.
Not the evidence.
The presence.

Because presence does something proof alone can't do.

Presence tells your nervous system: You are safe.
Presence tells your heart: You are not alone.
Presence tells your spirit: God is not avoiding you.

And in that moment, all the words I had been holding back came rushing forward—not as a rehearsed confession, but as a recognition that took over my whole body:

My Lord and my God.

I didn't say it like a theologian.

I said it like a man who had been afraid to hope and suddenly realized hope was standing right in front of him.

If you are in a season where you cannot see God, hear this:

God is not offended by your need for reassurance.

He is not intimidated by your questions.
He is not threatened by your honesty.
He is not distant because you are struggling.

Sometimes the most faithful thing you can do is stay within reach.

To keep showing up.
To keep praying small prayers.
To keep walking with God's people even when you feel different.
To keep your heart open just enough to say, "If You're here… help me see You."

God can handle the sentence you're afraid to pray.

And when He comes—whether through Scripture, through community, through quiet clarity, through a moment of undeniable peace—He will not come to shame you.

He will come with peace.

Because God doesn't only meet the confident.

He meets the cautious too.

He meets the bruised.
He meets the tired.
He meets the ones who say, "I want to believe, but I need help."

And that help is often not a lightning bolt.

It's a hand extended in the fog.

The Gentle Truth

Doubt is not always rebellion. Sometimes it is grief, fear, or trauma trying to protect what is tender.

God is not threatened by your questions. He can meet you with reassurance and peace, and He often speaks the language your heart can understand.

If you cannot believe without proof right now, stay within reach. Presence changes what arguments cannot.

A Small Practice for the Valley

If you're struggling to believe, try this "within reach" practice for the next week:

1) Pray one honest sentence each day:
"God, help me see You."

2) Stay connected to one safe faith rhythm:
- one Psalm,
- one short walk with prayer,
- one conversation with a trusted believer,
- or one quiet moment in worship music.

3) Write down one sign of peace you notice—no matter how small.

Prayer:

"Jesus, I want to believe.
Meet me where I am.
Give me peace in the fog.
Hold my faith until it strengthens."

Chapter Fifteen

When the Wound Came from Inside the Church

This chapter explores Paul—
for anyone wounded by God's people,
and needs the Shepherd who says, "I Myself will care for you."

I expected opposition from the outside.

That part didn't surprise me.

When you choose a life shaped by conviction, you learn early how to stand against criticism, hostility, even danger. You brace yourself for resistance from people who don't share your values or your faith.

What I was not prepared for was the pain that would come from inside.

From people who spoke the same language of belief.
From people who prayed the same prayers.
From people who claimed the same Lord.

That kind of wound lands differently.

It doesn't just hurt your feelings.
It shakes your trust.
It makes you question your discernment.

It leaves you wondering whether you were foolish to believe people would be safe.

I gave my life to building communities rooted in love, truth, and freedom.

And still—I was misunderstood.

Misrepresented.
Undermined.
Abandoned.

Some people walked away quietly.
Some spoke against me loudly.
Some questioned my motives.
Some distorted my words.

And a few—this part is the hardest—were people I had poured myself into.

I don't say this to paint the church as hopeless. I say it because I want you to know you are not alone if you've been wounded in a place you expected to be safe.

There is a special kind of confusion when spiritual harm happens.

When Scripture is quoted but compassion is missing.
When leadership speaks "vision" but forgets people.
When the crowd applauds the platform while someone quietly bleeds in the pews.

When “for the sake of the ministry” becomes a way to ignore what is right.

That kind of hurt tangles itself around your faith.

And if you’re not careful, it can make you think God is like the people who failed you.

But God is not synonymous with the people who misrepresented Him.

I had to learn that the hard way.

There were times I felt profoundly alone.

Not because I lacked community.
Because I had been wounded by it.

Some wounds were public.
Some were whispered.
Some were the slow erosion of trust—little dismissals, little manipulations, little moments where I realized love had become conditional.

And then there were the betrayals that still sting when I remember them.

A co-worker who left and never looked back.
A friend who chose comfort over loyalty.
A man who actively worked against me.

I remember writing words I never wanted to write: "At my first defense, no one stood with me, but all deserted me."

That sentence doesn't come from a man who never loved the church.

It comes from a man who did.

The valley of church hurt is not only about losing people.
It can be about losing identity.

You can build your life around "what you do for God"—your role, your calling, your position—and then one change, one decision, one shift in leadership, and suddenly the ground disappears.

You lose the community.
You lose the job.
You lose the support system.
You lose the mission you thought you'd carry forever.

And if your identity was wrapped around what you did, you can feel like you lost yourself too.

In that valley, God can feel distant—not because you stopped believing, but because everything that helped you feel connected has been removed.

So what do you do when the wound came from inside?

You let God become your Shepherd again.

Not a concept.
Not a slogan.
A Shepherd.

Long before my time, God spoke through a prophet about leaders who used people instead of loving them—shepherds who fed themselves while the sheep scattered. God didn't ignore that harm. He named it. He confronted it.

And then He made a promise that has steadied countless hearts:

"I Myself will search for My sheep and look after them… I will tend them… I will bind up the injured and strengthen the weak."

Do you hear it?

When human shepherds fail, God does not abandon the flock.

He steps in personally.

He says, in effect: "I will be your Shepherd. I will lead you. I will gather you. I will protect you. I will heal you."

That promise changes the valley.

Because it means your care is not ultimately dependent on one leader.
Your belonging is not ultimately dependent on one church.
Your future is not ultimately dependent on one role.

God Himself takes responsibility for your soul.

This does not excuse what happened.
This does not minimize the harm.
This does not rush your healing.

But it anchors you to something stronger than the institution that failed you:

The Shepherd who does not fail.

I learned to separate God's voice from harmful voices.

That is not easy, because spiritual harm often borrows God's name.

But over time—slowly, tenderly—God rebuilt my trust.

Not by forcing me back into unsafe spaces.
By shepherding me with patience.

He gave me boundaries without guilt.
He gave me discernment without cynicism.
He gave me community again—safe people, steady love, quiet faithfulness.

And yes—I kept going.

Not because people suddenly became perfect.

Because God remained faithful.

If you are walking through church hurt right now—if your faith feels bruised because of how someone treated you in God's name—hear this clearly:

Walking away from harm is not walking away from God.

Taking time to heal is not failure.

Questioning what wounded you does not make you faithless.

God sees your pain.
He knows the confusion.
He understands the hesitation.

And He is patient with your process.

You do not have to force yourself back into unsafe spaces to prove devotion.

You are allowed to heal.
You are allowed to grieve.
You are allowed to rebuild trust slowly.

God is not limited to one community.
He is not confined to one leader.
He is not threatened by your honesty.

He will shepherd you personally.

And in time, He will show you how to love again without losing yourself.

A Note for Your Story

Sometimes this valley is not theoretical. It is devastatingly practical: a leadership change, a job loss, a community fractured, a calling that suddenly feels taken from you. If you have ever lost your church, your role, your support system, and the sense of who you are because what you did for God was tied to your identity—this chapter is for you.

God's promise in Ezekiel 34 is not sentimental. It is a declaration of personal care: when others fail, God is strong. He is not waiting for you to "move on." He is gathering you, healing you, and reminding you that you are precious to Him—not for what you do, but for who you are as His beloved.

The Gentle Truth

Church wounds cut deeply because they tangle pain with faith. But God is not synonymous with the people who hurt you.

Healing may require distance, boundaries, and time. God does not rush that process.

And when human shepherds fail, God Himself promises to shepherd you—personally, tenderly, faithfully.

A Small Practice for the Valley

If you've been hurt in a faith community, try this gentle practice:

1) Name the wound honestly.
2) Ask God to separate His voice from harmful voices.
3) Choose one safe spiritual rhythm (prayer, Scripture, nature, silence).

Prayer:

"God, I was hurt in Your name.
Help me see You clearly again.
Shepherd me personally.
Heal what was wounded.
Guide me toward what is safe and true."

Chapter Sixteen

When Your Body Becomes the Valley

This chapter explores the woman who suffered for twelve years—
for anyone whose body has become the valley,
and needs dignity, belonging, and peace from Jesus.

I stopped counting the years after a while.

At first I counted everything—months, weeks, days—because counting felt like control. If I could measure the suffering, maybe I could manage it. Maybe I could explain it. Maybe I could convince myself it had an ending I could predict.

But suffering does not always respect calendars.

So eventually, I stopped counting and started enduring.

Twelve years is a long time to bleed.

It is a long time to wake up tired.
A long time to plan your day around weakness.
A long time to wonder if your body will ever feel like home again.

And it wasn't only the physical pain.

It was what the pain did to my life.

Chronic illness doesn't just hurt—it shrinks you.

It narrows your world to what you can handle.
It takes energy you didn't know you needed.
It steals spontaneity.
It steals confidence.
It steals the simple joy of waking up and not thinking about your body.

And then there was the social cost.

In my world, my condition made me "unclean."

That word is heavy.

It wasn't simply a medical reality—it became a spiritual label people used to keep distance. It made others cautious around me, as if my weakness could contaminate their safety. It put me on the outside of gatherings, the outside of worship, the outside of community.

Imagine being lonely in a crowd because you don't belong in it.

Imagine wanting God and feeling like you have to stay far back because your body has become a barrier.

That's what the valley felt like for me.

Not only pain.
Not only fatigue.
But separation.

I tried everything I could try.

I spent money I didn't have.
I trusted people I shouldn't have trusted.
I followed advice that promised relief and delivered disappointment.

One treatment after another.
One hope after another.

And instead of getting better, I grew worse.

That is a particular kind of grief: when you keep trying and the trying itself becomes exhausting.

And in time, the disappointment begins to press on your spirit.

You start asking questions you never wanted to ask:

Why won't God heal me?
Am I being punished?
Did I do something wrong?
Will I live like this forever?

Chronic illness can make you feel invisible—even to God—because the suffering is so steady it becomes background noise. And background noise is easy for other people to ignore.

But you cannot ignore your own body.

Every day, it is with you.

And some days, it feels like the body is the battlefield and you are losing.

Then I heard about Him.

People spoke His name the way thirsty people speak about water.

They said He healed.
They said He noticed the unnoticed.
They said He touched what others avoided.
They said He spoke with authority and tenderness braided together.

At first, I didn't let myself hope too much.

Because hope had hurt me before.

But something in me—something stubborn and small—refused to die.

So I went.

Not boldly.

Carefully.

Because when you've been dismissed for years, you learn how to move quietly through spaces that weren't built for you.

The crowd was thick. People pressed in around Him like waves. Everyone wanted something: a miracle, an answer, a moment of closeness.

And I remember thinking: There is no way I will get to Him.

Not like this.

Not with my weakness.

But the valley does something to you.

It makes you desperate enough to try what you would normally be too polite to do.

So I made a decision that felt both daring and fragile:

If I can just touch Him…

Not even speak.
Not even ask.
Just touch.

Maybe that's where you are too.

Maybe you don't have words right now.
Maybe you don't have energy for long prayers.
Maybe your faith feels like a thread.

But you can reach.

So I reached.

I slipped through the crowd like a whisper and extended my hand toward the hem of His garment—the edge, the fringe, the smallest point of contact.

And the moment my fingers touched cloth, something shifted inside my body like light moving through darkness.

The bleeding stopped.

Not slowly.
Not gradually.

Stopped.

My breath caught in my throat.

Relief flooded me so fast I almost collapsed.

For a second, I thought: I can disappear now. I can go home. No one has to know. I don't have to be seen.

Because when you've been ashamed for years, being healed can feel safer than being known.

But He stopped.

In the middle of the crowd, He stopped.

And He asked a question that made the whole moment terrifying:

"Who touched Me?"

My heart pounded.

Because if I stepped forward, I would be exposed.

I would be visible.
I would be named.
I would be a person again, not a problem.

And I feared what visibility might cost.

But He waited.

Not like someone angry.
Like someone attentive.

And I realized the question wasn't meant to shame me.

It was meant to restore me.

He wasn't only healing my body.

He was healing my belonging.

So I came forward trembling.

I told Him the truth.

All of it.

The years.
The loss.
The desperation.
The touch.

And He didn't recoil.

He didn't scold me for breaking social rules.
He didn't call me unclean.
He didn't tell me I should have stayed back.

He looked at me like I mattered.

And then He spoke one word that undid twelve years of loneliness:

"Daughter."

Not "patient."
Not "problem."
Not "woman."

Daughter.

Do you hear what He was doing?

He was giving me identity before giving me instruction.

He was placing me in a family before sending me into the future.

And then He said I could go in peace.

Peace.

Not only relief.
Peace.

Because the valley of chronic illness is not only physical. It is emotional and spiritual too. It makes your nervous system live on alert. It makes your heart brace for disappointment.

And Jesus did not only stop the bleeding.

He brought peace to the parts of me that had been bracing for years.

If your body has become the valley—if you're living with sickness, chronic pain, fatigue, disease, or the slow grief of a body that won't cooperate—hear this:

God sees you.

Not as a project.
Not as a burden.
Not as a spiritual problem.

As beloved.

And whether healing comes quickly, slowly, or in ways you cannot yet imagine, His presence is not dependent on your strength.

You do not have to fight your way into God's attention.

You only have to reach.

He is near enough for the smallest touch.

And He is gentle enough to meet you with dignity.

Even in the body-valley.
Even in the long years.
Even in the days you cannot see Him.

He is still here.

The Gentle Truth

Chronic illness can shrink your world and make you feel separated—from people, from worship, even from yourself.

But Jesus does not treat suffering bodies as inconveniences. He restores dignity and belonging, not just symptoms.

You are not invisible to God. You are not disqualified by weakness. You are beloved.

A Small Practice for the Valley

If your body feels overwhelmed today, try this gentle "one-touch prayer":

Place your hand on your chest (or anywhere that feels comforting).
Breathe slowly and whisper:

"Jesus, I reach for You. Meet me with peace.
Hold my body. Hold my heart.
Give me the next small step."

Then do one kind thing for your body today (as you are able):

- drink water,
- take medication as prescribed,
- rest without guilt,
- ask for help,
- or step into sunlight for one minute.

Chapter Seventeen

When You're Carrying Someone Else

This chapter explores Ruth—
for anyone carrying someone else's pain and feeling yourself disappear, and needs daily bread and permission to receive care too.

I didn't plan to become a caregiver.

I planned to have a normal life.

I planned for laughter and routine and the ordinary comfort of predictable days. I planned for the kind of future that doesn't require bravery. I planned for my life to feel… simple.

Then grief arrived at our door.

Not a small grief.

The kind that empties a house.

And suddenly, everything became about survival.

Two funerals can change a person.
Three can change a family.
And when the losses keep stacking, you stop asking "Why?" and start asking "How?"

How do we eat?
How do we stay safe?
How do we keep going?

I watched someone I loved lose everything.

Not dramatically.
Not all at once.
But steadily—like a light dimming day by day.

And the hardest part was that grief didn't only take what she had.

It took who she thought she was.

There are people who survive tragedy and still have a sense of direction.
And then there are people who survive tragedy and feel like they can't find themselves again.

That's what I witnessed.

She became sharp sometimes.
Not because she was cruel.
Because sorrow can harden the edges of a person who is trying not to fall apart.

Her words turned heavy.
Her hope turned quiet.
Her future turned gray.

And I understood.

Because when you're carrying grief, gentleness can feel like extra weight.

So when the moment came for me to choose my path—when I had every reasonable excuse to walk away—I found myself doing something I didn't expect.

I stayed.

People often romanticize loyalty, but I want you to hear the truth:

Staying was not poetic.

Staying was costly.

It meant leaving my familiar place.
It meant stepping into uncertainty.
It meant choosing a future where I couldn't guarantee provision, comfort, or safety.

It meant tying my life to someone else's pain and saying, "Your story will not be carried alone."

Caregiving can look like many things.

Sometimes it is physical care—appointments, medications, fatigue, meals.

Sometimes it is emotional care—listening, absorbing, making room for grief that needs somewhere to land.

Sometimes it is relational care—staying when others pull away, being the steady presence when someone's world has been shaken.

Often, it is all three at once.

And it can make you feel like you are disappearing.

Because when you carry someone else, your own needs can begin to feel less important.

You stop noticing your hunger.
You stop noticing your loneliness.
You stop noticing the places in your heart that ache, because all your attention is focused on keeping someone else afloat.

You become strong by necessity, and then one day you realize you have no idea how to rest.

You are tired, but you keep moving.
You are overwhelmed, but you keep showing up.
You are grieving too, but you push it aside because someone else's grief feels bigger.

This is a valley many people don't name.

The caregiver valley.

It isn't always dramatic.
It's daily.

It's the slow grind of responsibility.
The steady pressure of being needed.
The constant low hum of: Don't fall apart. They need you.

And in that valley, God can feel distant—not because you don't love Him, but because your life leaves no space to feel anything.

You can pray while washing dishes.
You can pray while driving.
You can pray while holding someone else's hand in a waiting room.

But those prayers can feel thin.

Because caregiving is a full-body assignment.

And sometimes your spirit feels like it's living on scraps.

I want you to know this:

God sees caregiving.

He sees the unseen labor.
He sees the invisible sacrifices.
He sees the nights you stayed awake.
He sees the decisions you made that no one applauded.
He sees the moments you swallowed your own tears so someone else could cry.

And God is not only grateful.

He is present.

In my story, provision did not arrive as a grand miracle.

It arrived in ordinary ways.

A field that offered leftovers.
A community that noticed.
A man who treated us with dignity.
Small mercies stacked day after day until the fog began to lift.

And I learned something about God in the caregiver valley:

God does not only care about the one you are carrying.

He also cares about you.

You are not a supporting character to God.
You are not invisible because you are quiet.
You are not less important because your love looks like work.

In fact, sometimes love looks exactly like work.

Love looks like staying.
Love looks like showing up.

Love looks like doing the next right thing on a day when your heart is tired.

And God honors that kind of love.

Not by demanding more from you.

But by meeting you with daily bread.

By giving strength you didn't know you had.
By providing help you didn't know was coming.
By reminding you that your faithfulness is seen—even when it feels small.

If you are carrying someone else right now—an aging parent, a sick spouse, a struggling child, a friend in crisis—hear this:

You are not alone.

God is not asking you to burn out to prove devotion.

He is inviting you into a rhythm of care that includes you.

He can give you permission to rest.
He can give you courage to ask for help.
He can give you wisdom to set boundaries.
He can give you strength for today—only today—so you don't have to carry tomorrow in your arms too.

In the caregiver valley, God often leads one day at a time.

And that is enough.

Because the Shepherd does not only watch the flock.

He watches the one who is doing the carrying.

The Gentle Truth

Caregiving can make you feel like you're disappearing, but God sees your unseen labor. He cares for the one you are carrying—and He cares for you.

You are allowed to need help. You are allowed to rest. You are allowed to set boundaries without guilt.

A Small Practice for the Valley

If you are caregiving, try this simple daily rhythm:

1) Morning: "God, give me today's strength."
2) Midday: Ask one small help (a call, a meal, a ride, a break).
3) Evening: Name one mercy you noticed.

Prayer:

"God, I feel tired. I feel needed.
Meet me with daily bread.
Show me where I can rest.
Help me receive care too."

Chapter Eighteen

When You Feel Misunderstood

This chapter explores Hannah—
for anyone misunderstood in your grief,
and needs to know God hears prayers with no words.

If you had seen me in the sanctuary, you might have thought I was fine.

I looked like anyone else—standing among people, present in body, moving through the familiar motions of worship. Nothing about my posture would have told you that my heart was breaking.

But inside, I was unraveling.

There is a kind of pain that doesn't show up on your face until it finally does—and even then, people often misread it.

They assume it's drama.
They assume it's weakness.
They assume it's attention-seeking.

But some grief is not performed.

Some grief is swallowed.

And that was me.

I carried a longing I could not fix.

Year after year, month after month, I held the same ache: I wanted a child.

Not as a symbol.
Not as a story.
As a real life.

In my world, barrenness was not just personal sadness—it was a label people felt comfortable attaching to your identity. It invited whispers. It invited advice. It invited pity that didn't feel like kindness.

And it invited mockery.

There was a woman who made sure my wound stayed open.

Some people are like that. They poke what hurts—not because they understand, but because your pain makes them feel powerful.

Her words were sharp.
Her presence was heavy.
Her joy felt like salt in my mouth.

And I tried to keep it together.

I tried to be polite.
I tried to be faithful.
I tried to act like I was unbothered.

But you can only carry silent sorrow for so long before it begins to leak out of you.

That day, I couldn't hold it anymore.

The longing, the shame, the jealousy, the disappointment, the exhaustion of pretending—it all rose up like a wave I could not stop.

So I went to the house of God.

Not because I felt holy.

Because I had nowhere else to put my pain.

I didn't come with a speech.
I didn't come with a polished prayer.

I came with tears.

My lips moved, but my voice didn't come out.

I didn't have the strength for performative religion.
I didn't have the energy to pray like someone who wasn't hurting.

So I prayed the way people pray when they're desperate.

Silently.
Messily.
Honestly.

I wasn't trying to impress God.

I was trying to survive.

Then a man approached me—a leader, a priest, a person who should have recognized grief.

Instead, he judged me.

He looked at my silent tears and assumed the worst.

He saw my trembling and decided it meant I was faithless. He saw my intensity and decided it meant I was out of control.

He accused me of being drunk.

Do you know what it feels like to be misunderstood when you are already in pain?

It feels like being pushed underwater.

Because you are drowning, and someone stands over you insisting you're the problem.

That accusation could have crushed me.

But something in me—something tired and true—rose up.

I told him the truth.

I am not what you think I am.

I am a woman with a heavy heart.

That sentence was my lifeline.

Because naming the truth is sometimes the only way to keep your dignity in the valley.

And to his credit, he listened.

He softened.
He blessed me.
He spoke peace over me.

But I need you to understand something:

Even if he had not listened, God already had.

God did not misread my tears.

God did not mistake my grief for rebellion.
God did not confuse my silence for distance of heart.

He saw me.

That is what changes you in the valley of misunderstanding.

Not people finally "getting it."
But God seeing you clearly.

I walked out of that place different—not because my situation had changed in an instant, but because something inside me had shifted.

Hope returned.

Not loud hope.
Quiet hope.

The kind that doesn't guarantee an outcome but allows you to breathe again.

Because being seen by God gives you strength to keep living even when the longing remains.

If you have ever been misunderstood—especially by people who should have known better—hear this:

God is not confused about you.

He knows what is grief and what is rebellion.
He knows what is honest struggle and what is hardened refusal.
He knows what is exhaustion and what is indifference.

Your tears are not suspicious to Him.

Your silence is not offensive to Him.

And your pain does not make you a problem to be managed.

Sometimes the most spiritual thing you can do is what I did:

Show up as you are.
Tell the truth.
Pour out your heart.
Refuse to let someone else's misreading define you.

God hears the prayers you cannot speak out loud.

He hears the ones that come out as tears.

And He is gentle with the misunderstood.

I learned that the valley can be holy ground—not because the pain is good, but because God meets you there.

He met me.

And He will meet you too.

The Gentle Truth

Being misunderstood can make pain feel heavier—especially when it comes from people who should have been safe.

But God does not misread you. He understands your tears, your silence, and your longing with compassion.

You are not defined by someone else's misinterpretation. You are seen clearly by God.

A Small Practice for the Valley

If you feel misunderstood, try this:

1) Name the truth in one sentence:
"God, I feel misread."

2) Tell God what is actually happening inside you (three honest phrases):
"I feel ______."
"I fear ______."
"I need ______."

3) Choose one boundary that protects your tenderness today:
• step back from an unsafe conversation,
• reach out to one safe person,
• or give yourself permission to be quiet.

Prayer:

"God, You see me.
Hold my heart.
Help me live in truth—not in others' assumptions."

Chapter Nineteen

When Your Story Has a Reputation

This chapter explores the Samaritan woman—
for anyone whose story has a reputation,
and needs living water and truth without disgust.

People can decide who you are before you ever open your mouth.

They can take pieces of your story—fragments, headlines, whispers—and turn them into a label that follows you like a shadow.

And once you've been labeled, it can feel like the world only sees the label.

Not your heart.
Not your longing.
Not your wounds.
Not the complexity of how you got there.

Just the reputation.

I know what that is like.

I didn't set out to become "that kind of woman."

I didn't wake up one day and decide, I want my life to be a cautionary talc.

My story became what it became because of a thousand small moments—needs I didn't know how to name, choices I made in survival, relationships that promised belonging and delivered emptiness.

And yes, some of it was my own doing.

That's the part you have to hold honestly.

But some of it was also the world I lived in—what women had to do to survive, what we had access to, what we didn't. People love simple narratives because they make judgment easier.

But real lives are rarely simple.

By the time my story settled into its reputation, I had learned how to live with eyes on me.

Not kind eyes.

The kind that scan you for evidence.
The kind that assume the worst.
The kind that treat you like a moral lesson instead of a person.

So I stopped expecting tenderness from people.

I learned to keep my distance.
To stay guarded.
To take what I could get and not ask for more.

And then, as if my reputation wasn't enough, my life became unstable.

My relationships were unstable.
My sense of home was unstable.
Even my worship life felt unstable—because it's hard to feel close to God when you're convinced you're too far gone.

But you still get thirsty.

That's what surprises people about the broken.

We still get thirsty.

We still want love.
We still want peace.
We still want a life that doesn't feel like we're always starting over.

So I came to the well in the middle of the day.

Not because I liked the heat.

Because I didn't want the looks.

Morning and evening were crowded—women talking, laughing, comparing stories, scanning each other's lives for reasons to feel superior.

I didn't have the strength for that.

So I came when no one would be there.

Or so I thought.

He was there.

Sitting.
Waiting.
As if He had planned to meet me.

He was a Jewish man. I was a Samaritan woman. We didn't cross those lines. Not socially. Not safely.

And yet He spoke to me like I was human.

He asked for water.

At first, I thought it was strange.

Then I realized: He was offering me something too.

Because there is a way God approaches you that disarms shame.

Not by pretending you don't have a past.
By meeting you like your past isn't the whole truth about you.

He told me He could give living water.

And I wanted it immediately—because thirst makes you impulsive.

"Give me this water," I said, "so I don't have to keep coming here."

Do you hear what I was really saying?

I don't want this life anymore.
I don't want this cycle anymore.
I don't want this shame anymore.
I don't want this lonely walk in the heat anymore.

And then He did something that made my stomach drop.

He asked me about my life.

Not to shame me.

To show me that He already knew.

There is a moment in the valley when you realize God isn't guessing about you.

He isn't piecing your story together from rumors.

He knows the truth—every chapter.

And when He named what He knew, it felt like exposure at first.

Because exposure is terrifying when you've been surviving on hiding.

But His eyes weren't accusing.

His voice wasn't cruel.

He spoke the truth without disgust.

That is rare.

That is holy.

It was the first time I realized: I can be fully known and not rejected.

And something in me shifted.

Not because I became instantly perfect.

Because I became seen.

That's what repentance often begins as: not self-hatred, but clarity. Not punishment, but awakening.

I tried to change the subject—people do that when they're uncomfortable. I tried to turn it into a theological debate, because theology can become a shield when your heart is exposed.

But He stayed gentle.

He stayed present.

And then He did the unthinkable.

He revealed Himself to me.

Not to the powerful.
Not to the polished.
Not to the people with clean reputations.

To me.

A woman in the heat with a complicated story.

He let me see Him.

And once I saw Him, I couldn't unsee Him.

I left my water jar—the thing I had come for—and ran back to people I had been avoiding.

That's how you know something real happened.

Shame makes you hide.
Encounter makes you move.

I told them what happened.

Not as a performance.
As a confession mixed with hope:

He knew me… and He stayed.

If your story has a reputation—if you've been labeled, reduced, dismissed, or treated like your past is the only thing you are—hear this:

Jesus does not love you from a distance.

He meets you in the heat.
He meets you at the well.
He meets you in the place you go to avoid being seen.

And He tells the truth—not to crush you, but to free you.

Your past may be real.
Your consequences may be real.
Your regret may be real.

But your reputation is not your identity.

When Jesus names you, you become more than what people whispered.

You become beloved.

And that belovedness is the beginning of a new story.

The Gentle Truth

Shame reduces you to your past, but Jesus sees your whole story with compassion.

He tells the truth without disgust. He offers living water to people with complicated reputations.

You are not defined by what people call you. You are defined by what Jesus calls you: beloved.

A Small Practice for the Valley

If shame or reputation is heavy right now, try this:

1) Name the label you've been carrying.
2) Replace it with a truth Jesus would speak.

Example:
"I am ruined" → "I am seen and still loved."

Prayer:

"Jesus, meet me in the place I hide.
Tell me the truth with gentleness.
Give me living water—new desire, new courage, a new story."

Chapter Twenty

When You Love Someone You Can't Control

This chapter explores the father who waited—for anyone who loves someone you can't control, and needs strength to wait with wisdom and tenderness.

I watched the road more than anyone knew.

Not in an obvious way.

I didn't stand at the edge of the property every day like a statue of longing. I had responsibilities. I had work. I had a household to manage. Life did not stop simply because my heart was waiting.

But there was a part of me—quiet, constant—that always listened for footsteps that weren't there.

Because when someone you love walks away, a strange kind of waiting begins.

Waiting that isn't passive.
Waiting that aches.
Waiting that keeps a light on in places you pretend are dark.

He left with confidence.

That's what hurt the most in the beginning: how sure he was.

He wanted his inheritance early—his future in his hands right now. He wanted freedom the way young people often want it: as distance from authority, distance from responsibility, distance from anyone who might say, "Are you sure?"

I could have refused him.

People assume that is what love should do—tighten the grip when someone is headed toward harm.

But love is not always control.

Sometimes love is the painful dignity of letting someone choose.

I gave him what he asked for.

Not because it didn't hurt.
Because I would not turn my son into a prisoner just to ease my anxiety.

And when he walked away, it felt like a door closing in my chest.

There are losses that come with funerals, and there are losses that come with departure.

Departure loss is strange because the person is still alive, but they are not with you.

You don't get the finality of grief.
You get the uncertainty of hope.

You wonder where they are.
You wonder who they're with.
You wonder what they're doing.
You wonder if they are safe.
You wonder if they are eating.
You wonder if they think of home.
You wonder if they hate you.
You wonder if you failed.

Parenting pain is unique.

Because you can't fix it.
You can't take the consequences for them.
You can't make choices on their behalf.

You can only love.

And love can feel powerless when you're watching someone self-destruct.

I did what I could do.

I prayed.
I listened.
I waited.
I kept the household steady.
I tried not to let bitterness set in.

But I won't pretend it was easy.

There were nights I lay awake imagining every possible outcome, because your mind will try to solve what your heart cannot control.

There were days I felt anger—anger at his choices, anger at the waste, anger at the way he treated love like something disposable.

There were days I felt shame—because people judge parents when children go wild. They assume it means the home was broken, the father was absent, the family was weak.

They rarely understand that children can be deeply loved and still choose pain.

And then there was the temptation to harden.

To protect myself by deciding ahead of time:

If he comes back, I will make him pay.
If he returns, I will remind him.
If he shows up, I will keep my distance.

Hardness feels like safety.

But it is expensive.

Because the moment you decide you will not be moved by love again, you lose something of yourself.

So I tried to stay tender.

Not foolish.
Tender.

I held boundaries in my heart:
I would not chase him into his destruction.
I would not enable.
I would not pretend choices don't matter.

But I would not stop being his father.

I would not stop hoping.
I would not stop watching the road.

And then—one day—I saw someone.

Far off.

A figure moving slowly, like the ground was heavy under him.

My heart recognized him before my mind did.

There is a kind of knowing that lives deeper than logic.

I knew.

And my body moved before my pride could speak.

I ran.

Men like me did not run.

Dignity doesn't run.
Status doesn't run.
Respect doesn't run.

But love runs.

I ran because my son was coming home.
I ran because the waiting was ending.
I ran because the road that took him away was finally bringing him back.

When I reached him, he started speaking—the speech he had rehearsed, the words he had prepared to earn a small corner of mercy.

But I didn't need the speech.

I could see it on him—the hunger, the regret, the humiliation, the exhaustion of carrying consequences.

He didn't need a lecture first.

He needed a father.

So I held him.

And in that embrace, I was making a statement the whole village could see:

This one belongs.

Do you know why that mattered?

Because return is fragile.

The first moments home can determine whether someone stays or runs again.

Shame is loud at the doorway.

So I made mercy louder.

I called for a robe.
A ring.
Sandals.

Belonging.
Identity.
Freedom.

Then I did something that still surprises people:

I celebrated.

Not because what he did was okay.
Not because consequences were imaginary.
Not because repentance cancels reality.

I celebrated because my son was alive.

And sometimes, in parenting valleys, the victory is not perfection.

It's return.

It's one step toward home.
One conversation.
One softened heart.
One day sober.

One phone call.
One honest apology.
One willingness to try again.

If you are loving someone you cannot control—if you are waiting for a child, a spouse, a sibling, a friend—hear this:

You are not powerless.

Love is not powerless.

It is patient.
It is steady.
It is wise.
It holds boundaries.
It keeps the door open without throwing yourself into the fire.

God understands this kind of love.

Because God loves us that way.

He does not enable.
He does not pretend our drift is harmless.
He does not erase consequences like they don't matter.

But He watches.
He waits.
He runs toward return.

So take heart.

Your waiting is not wasted.
Your prayers are not forgotten.
Your tenderness is not foolish.

Keep watching the road—but don't lose yourself on it.

Let God hold you while you love them.

Because you cannot control another person's choices, but you can remain a steady place of love when they are ready to come home.

And if they aren't ready yet—if the road is still long—God is still with you in the waiting.

The Gentle Truth

Loving someone you can't control can feel unbearable. Waiting can turn into anxiety, shame, or hardness.

But love does not have to become enabling. Love can hold boundaries and still keep a door open.

God understands the ache of waiting—and He is with you on the road.

A Small Practice for the Valley

If you're waiting for someone you love, try this three-part practice:

1) Release what you can't control:
"God, I cannot choose for them."

2) Ask for wise love:
"Teach me boundaries that protect, and mercy that stays tender."

3) Take one care step for yourself today:

- eat a meal,
- take a walk,
- talk with a trusted friend or counselor,
- or set one boundary that reduces chaos.

Prayer:

"Father, keep my heart soft.
Keep me wise.
Hold my waiting.
And when return comes, help me be ready with love."

Chapter Twenty-One

When Doing the Right Thing Still Costs You

This chapter explores Daniel—
for anyone doing the right thing and still paying the price, and needs steadiness when the system is unfair.

I was careful.

Not fearful—careful.

When you live long enough in a system that can turn on you, you learn the difference between wisdom and paranoia. Wisdom watches the room without losing peace. Wisdom keeps your hands clean, your words honest, and your heart steady—even when the politics around you are loud.

That was how I lived.

I did my work well.

Not to impress.
Not to advance.
Not to make a name for myself.

Because faithfulness matters—even when no one applauds it.

I served under leaders who did not share my convictions. I worked inside systems that were not built to protect people like me. I navigated cultures, expectations, and court intrigue that could swallow a person whole if they weren't grounded.

And for a long time, integrity brought favor.

People trusted me.
They placed responsibility in my hands.
They relied on my judgment.

It would be comforting if the story ended there—if doing right always led to safety.

But life doesn't always work that way.

There came a season when my consistency made me a target.

Not because I changed.
Because the environment did.

Jealousy arrived.

Quiet at first—side glances, tightened smiles, conversations that stopped when I entered the room. Then it became more direct: criticism disguised as concern, suspicion dressed up as "accountability," questions meant to plant doubt rather than seek truth.

They wanted to find something real they could use against me.

Corruption.
Neglect.
Some hidden weakness.

But they couldn't.

My hands were clean.

And when people can't find fault in your life, they sometimes create a reason to punish your faith.

That's what they did.

They watched me closely. They studied my habits. They learned my rhythms. They noticed the most consistent thing about my life:

I prayed.

Not to make a statement.
Not to perform devotion.
Not to prove anything.

I prayed because God was my anchor.

And in a world full of shifting loyalties, I needed something steady.

So they built a trap around my prayers.

That's how injustice often works.

It doesn't always look violent.
It looks official.

It hides behind policy.
It cloaks itself in procedure.
It wears the mask of "This is just how things are done."

They drafted a decree and convinced the king to sign it.

A law with polished words and cruel intent:

For a period of time, no one could pray to anyone except the king.

It sounded like unity.
Like loyalty.
Like national stability.

But it was worship disguised as governance.

And now my quiet devotion had become illegal.

I knew the cost.

This wasn't ignorance.
This wasn't naïveté.

This was clarity.

And clarity doesn't make the choice easier—it makes it heavier.

Because now I wasn't just deciding for myself. My decision would affect my position, my future, my safety. It would become public. It would become a story other people would tell.

So I went home.

I opened the windows the way I always had.

Not because I wanted attention.
Because hiding my devotion would have made fear my shepherd.

And I prayed.

Not loudly.
Not dramatically.

Faithfully.

I want you to notice that: my obedience did not look heroic on the outside.

It looked like consistency.

Sometimes the most courageous thing you will ever do is keep doing what is right when the consequences become real.

And the consequences came quickly.

They rushed to the king.
They framed it as rebellion.
They used the law like a weapon, pretending they

cared about order when what they really wanted was my removal.

The king was distressed.

He hadn't understood what he had signed.

He tried to find a way out—because sometimes even powerful leaders realize too late that they've been manipulated.

But the law stood.

And in the end, he ordered what he didn't want to order.

I was taken.

Do you know what it feels like to be punished for doing the right thing?

It is disorienting.

It makes your stomach twist.
It makes your mind race.
It makes your heart ask, again and again:

God, why would You let this happen?

Because somewhere deep down, many of us carry an unspoken equation:

If I obey God, things will work out.

But life doesn't always follow that math.

Sometimes obedience leads to loss.
Sometimes integrity leads to isolation.
Sometimes righteousness leads to the den.

That's the valley no one prepares you for.

The valley where faithfulness doesn't look rewarded.
The valley where God feels silent.
The valley where you wonder if integrity was worth it.

The stone rolled into place.
The opening sealed.
The darkness pressed in.

And that night, I learned something I will never forget:

God does not always rescue us from unjust spaces.
Sometimes He meets us inside them.

His presence was not loud.
It did not erase the danger.
But it steadied me.

And that steadiness mattered.

Because injustice tries to do more than harm your circumstances—it tries to corrode your soul.

It tries to make you bitter.
It tries to make you cynical.

It tries to convince you that goodness is foolish and faith is a liability.

But God kept my heart anchored.

Morning came.

And when the stone was moved and my name was called, I answered—alive.

The miracle was undeniable.

But hear me: the point of the story is not only that God shut lions' mouths.

The point is that God does not abandon His people when the system is unfair.

Even if the den had been my end, God would still have been good.

Because God's faithfulness is not measured by outcomes.
It is measured by presence.

If you are facing injustice—if you did the right thing and still paid the price—hear this:

God sees.

He sees the integrity no one applauded.
He sees the cost you absorbed.
He sees the way you stayed honest when compromise would have been easier.

He sees the sleepless nights and the anxious mornings.
He sees the quiet courage of choosing what is right again and again.

Justice may be delayed.

But your faithfulness is not wasted.

Sometimes God delivers quickly.
Sometimes He delivers slowly.
Sometimes He delivers in ways you did not expect.

But He does not forget.

And even when systems fail, God remains just.

So hold on.

You are not foolish for choosing integrity.
You are not abandoned because justice was delayed.
And you are not alone in the den.

God is still present.
God is still powerful.
God is still writing the story.

Even here.

The Gentle Truth

Injustice is especially painful when it comes as a consequence of faithfulness.

God sees integrity even when systems punish it. Your obedience is not invisible to Him, and His presence is not dependent on fair outcomes.

Even in the den, God can keep your soul steady.

A Small Practice for the Valley

If injustice has shaken you, try this grounding practice:

1) Name what was unjust (one sentence).
2) Name what you did right (one sentence).
3) Entrust the outcome to God (one sentence).

Prayer:

"God, You see what happened.
You know the truth.
Hold me steady while You work.
Protect me from bitterness.
Help me keep choosing what is right."

Chapter Twenty-Two

When You Can't Decide What to Do Next

**This chapter explores Gideon—
for anyone overwhelmed and unsure of the next step, and needs God's patient guidance one decision at a time.**

I wish I could tell you I was brave from the beginning.

That the moment God called my name, I stood up with confidence and clarity and said, "Yes. Of course. I'm ready."

But that wasn't me.

When God first came near, I wasn't standing on a platform. I was hiding—doing ordinary work in a way that kept me out of sight. It wasn't because I loved the shadows. It was because I was tired of being afraid.

The world around me had taught fear like it was a second language.

We lived under pressure—harvests stolen, families stressed, futures narrowed. We learned to plan for loss. We learned to store what we could and hope it lasted. We learned the subtle, exhausting art of staying small so no one would notice us.

That kind of environment doesn't just threaten your safety.

It reshapes your nervous system.

It trains you to expect disappointment.
To anticipate danger.
To assume that whatever you build will be taken.

And when you live that way long enough, decision-making becomes heavy.

Because every choice feels like a risk.
Every step forward feels like an invitation to get hurt.
Every "yes" feels like a setup.

So I became careful.

Not wise-careful.

Fear-careful.

I kept my expectations low so I wouldn't be crushed by hope again.

And then God spoke.

Not with thunder.
Not with the kind of voice that forces you to feel brave.

With a presence that felt steady.

He called me "mighty warrior."

I almost laughed.

Not because it was funny, but because it was impossible.

Mighty warriors don't hide.
Mighty warriors don't shrink.
Mighty warriors don't rehearse worst-case scenarios in their minds before breakfast.

So I answered Him the way overwhelmed people answer:

With questions.

If God is with us, why does it feel like we're losing?
Where are all the stories we grew up hearing—deliverance, provision, miracles?
And if You're really calling me… why me?

I didn't just feel unqualified.

I felt wrong for the assignment.

I had no confidence in myself.
No confidence in my family's status.
No confidence in my capacity.

And here is the part that still moves me:

God did not shame my questions.

He didn't call me weak for asking.
He didn't demand I pretend to be strong.

He simply said, “I will be with you.”

That should have been enough.

But anxiety doesn’t disappear just because truth is spoken.

Sometimes truth has to be repeated until your body believes it.

So God gave me something practical—a step.

And that step was… uncomfortable.

He told me to tear down what my people trusted instead of Him.

That wasn’t just spiritual.
That was social.
That was relational.
That was risky.

Because sometimes the next right step isn’t dramatic—it’s disruptive.

It threatens the false peace you’ve been using to survive.

So I did it at night.

I’m not proud of that.

But I’m honest.

I did it at night because fear still had a grip on me.

And yet—obedience still happened.

That mattered.

Because one of the most important things I learned in my valley is this:

God can work with trembling obedience.

He would rather have a fearful "yes" than a confident "later."

Then the next pressure arrived: a real battle. Real stakes. Real consequences.

People gathered. The moment became public. The decision wasn't theoretical anymore.

And my mind did what minds do when the stakes rise:

It spiraled.

What if I misheard?
What if I fail?
What if I make it worse?
What if I lead people into loss?
What if my fear is a sign God shouldn't have chosen me?

Decision fatigue doesn't always look like laziness.

It looks like paralysis.

It looks like staring at the same options until your thoughts blur.
It looks like wanting certainty and feeling unable to move without it.
It looks like your body bracing as if every choice might be a cliff.

That's where I was.

So I asked for reassurance.

More than once.

People have teased me for that ever since.

But God didn't.

God didn't say, "How dare you ask again?"
He didn't say, "Real faith wouldn't need this."

He met me.

Again.

And again.

He gave signs that were almost tender—simple confirmations that said, "I'm not asking you to imagine Me. I'm here."

Now, I need to say this clearly: God's patience with me was not an invitation to avoid growth forever.

It was God's kindness with a bruised spirit.

Because fear does not always vanish in a single prayer. Sometimes fear loosens its grip through repeated encounters with God's faithfulness.

And as I took small steps—imperfect, hesitant steps—something surprising happened:

Courage grew behind my obedience.

Not before I moved.

As I moved.

As I showed up.
As I took the next right step with shaking hands.
As I discovered God meets you on the way, not only at the destination.

Then came the strangest instruction of all.

God began to reduce the number of people who were going with me.

This felt backward.

When you feel overwhelmed, you want more support, more safety, more backup.

But God was doing something holy:

He was untangling my heart from the need to control outcomes.

He was teaching me that the battle wouldn't be won by numbers.
It would be won by trust.

This is where many of us struggle.

Because we want clarity, and we want guarantees, and we want the plan in writing.

But God often gives light like a lantern—enough for the next few steps, not enough for the whole road.

So I moved forward with what I had:

One promise.
One next step.
One day's courage.

And the fog lifted—not all at once, but enough.

Not enough to make me feel invincible.

Enough to make me faithful.

If you are decision-fatigued right now—if you are stuck, overwhelmed, unsure what to do next—hear this:

God is not disappointed in your humanity.

He does not require you to solve everything today.

He is not asking you to force clarity out of anxiety.

He is inviting you into a small, steady faith:

Ask.
Listen.
Take one step.

Even if it's tiny.

Because tiny steps still count as movement.

And movement in the direction of God—no matter how slow—brings you closer to peace.

Sometimes the miracle isn't that God suddenly makes everything clear.

Sometimes the miracle is that God walks with you through the unclear.

He steadies you.
He reassures you.
He teaches you how to trust Him one decision at a time.

And over time, you realize what I realized:

God can lead fearful people.

God can use hesitant people.

God can shepherd you through the valley of "I don't know what to do next."

And He can make your next step enough.

The Gentle Truth

Decision fatigue can feel like paralysis, especially when the future is unclear and the stakes feel high.

God is patient with trembling people. He can meet you with reassurance and give you the next small step.

You don't need the whole map today. You only need enough light for the next step.

A Small Practice for the Valley

If you feel stuck, try this "one-step discernment" practice:

1) Write down your options (keep it simple).
2) Ask God one question:
"What is the next right step—not the whole plan?"

3) Choose one small action you can take in the next 24 hours:
- make one phone call,
- gather one piece of information,
- schedule one appointment,
- or have one honest conversation.

Prayer:

"God, I feel overwhelmed.
Give me wisdom for one step.
Meet me on the way.
Grow my courage as I obey."

Chapter Twenty-Three

When Everyone Knows You Failed

This chapter explores Peter—
for anyone carrying public failure and private shame, and needs restoration that rebuilds life one step at a time.

It's one thing to fail privately.

It's another thing to fail publicly—where the moment becomes a story, and the story becomes a label, and the label follows you into every room.

I know that valley.

I didn't fail because I didn't love Him.

That's what still aches when I remember it.

I failed because I was afraid.

Because pressure does strange things to the human body. It tightens the throat. It makes the mind search for escape. It convinces you that survival is more important than truth.

And on that night, fear won.

I had promised I would stay.

I had meant it.

I had looked Jesus in the eye and said I would never deny Him. I wasn't performing. I wasn't trying to impress anyone. I truly believed my devotion would hold when everything around us fell apart.

But devotion and courage are not always the same thing.

Devotion can be sincere and still collapse under terror.

That's what happened.

The night was loud with chaos—torches, accusation, movement, danger. The air felt charged, like a storm was about to break. I followed at a distance because I wanted to stay near Him, but I didn't know how to be brave.

Distance felt like the safest version of loyalty I could manage.

Then someone recognized me.

Not with hatred—just recognition.

"You were with Him," they said.

My heart jumped.

Because in that moment, being "with Him" felt like a sentence.

So I did what fear told me to do.

I denied Him.

Once.
Then again.
Then again.

Three denials—each one more desperate than the last, because once you start lying to save yourself, you feel trapped in it.

And then the rooster crowed.

And Jesus looked at me.

That look wasn't rage.

It wasn't humiliation.

It was grief—grief and knowing.

The kind of knowing that sees past your brave words and recognizes your trembling humanity.

I walked out into the dark and wept.

Not polite tears.
Not quiet regret.

The kind of sobbing that empties a person.

Because I didn't only feel like I failed Jesus.

I felt like I discovered something about myself I didn't want to know.

That I was weaker than I thought.
That my courage was thinner than my confidence.
That my love—though real—was not enough to keep me from collapsing under pressure.

That is what public failure does.

It doesn't just embarrass you.
It exposes you.

And exposure can feel like the end of your story.

After His death, the shame got heavier.

I replayed the denials in my head like a punishment I couldn't stop administering.

I imagined His voice.
His hands.
His kindness.

And my cowardice in the face of it.

When He rose, the others ran toward the news with joy.

I ran toward it with a knot in my stomach.

Because resurrection is beautiful—unless you're the one who failed Him.

Then resurrection feels complicated.

It means He's alive… and now you have to face Him.

And if you're honest, that's what some of you are afraid of too.

Not that God exists—
but that He sees.

That He knows what you did.
That He remembers the moment you broke your own values.
That He witnessed the decision you wish you could erase.

Public failure creates a new fear:

Not just, "What will people think?"

But, "Will I ever be trusted again?"
"Will I ever be useful again?"
"Is my calling canceled?"
"Is my future compromised?"

After the denial, I didn't know how to lead.

I didn't know how to speak with authority when my own story contained cowardice.

So I went back to what I knew.

Fishing.

Some people call that regression.

But sometimes when you're ashamed, you return to what feels familiar because the future feels too big to step into.

We were out on the water when it happened.

A voice from the shore.
A suggestion.
A catch so abundant it felt like a memory coming alive.

My heart recognized Him before my mind could catch up.

And something in me broke open.

I threw myself into the water and swam to Him.

Not because I was confident.

Because I couldn't stay far away anymore.

He had a fire burning.

That detail mattered.

Because the last time I stood near a fire, I was denying Him.

Now He had built another one—almost like He was saying:

We're going to revisit the moment, but we're going to rewrite what shame tried to finalize.

He fed me first.

Before the conversation.
Before the restoration.
Before anything else.

He gave me breakfast like love does when it wants you to remember you are still family.

Then He asked me the question that had been waiting in the air since the rooster crowed.

"Do you love Me?"

Not, "Why did you do it?"
Not, "How could you?"
Not, "Explain yourself."

Do you love Me?

He asked three times.

Not to rub it in.

To heal it.

To match the denials with a new confession.

Three times my mouth spoke love over the place where fear had once spoken betrayal.

And then He did the part I didn't expect:

He entrusted me with people.

"Feed My sheep."

Do you understand what that means?

He didn't only forgive me.

He restored my calling.

Not because failure didn't matter.
Not because trust is cheap.
Not because consequences are imaginary.

But because grace is stronger than the chapter you wish you could erase.

He was teaching me something I needed to learn in my bones:

Your worst moment is not your final identity.

Your failure is not the end of your usefulness.
Your shame is not stronger than My love.
And your story is not defined by where you collapsed—
it's defined by where you return.

Now, I need to say this carefully—because restoration doesn't always mean you pick up exactly where you left off.

Sometimes rebuilding trust takes time.
Sometimes repair requires accountability.
Sometimes humility is the road back into leadership.

Sometimes stepping down is part of healing, not punishment.

But hear this clearly:

God's love does not cancel you because you fell.

He doesn't pretend the fall didn't happen.
He meets you in it.
He feeds you in it.
He restores you from it.

If you are in the valley of public failure—if people know, if you feel exposed, if you're ashamed, if you're wondering whether you'll ever be okay again—listen:

The Jesus who met me on the shore still meets people like us.

He is not afraid of the truth.
He is not startled by your collapse.
He is not interested in humiliating you.

He is interested in restoring you.

One honest confession at a time.
One repaired relationship at a time.
One step of integrity at a time.

And when He restores, it isn't to make you impressive again.

It's to make you whole.

So come to the fire.

Let Him feed you.

Let Him ask you the question that matters most—not as a test, but as a doorway:

Do you love Me?

Because love—returning love—is where your future begins.

The Gentle Truth

Public failure can feel like the end, but Jesus specializes in restoration. He does not minimize what happened, yet He does not reduce you to it.

Restoration may include accountability and time, but God's love is stronger than your worst chapter.

A Small Practice for the Valley

If you're carrying public shame, try this restoration practice:

1) Tell the truth to God (one sentence):
"Jesus, I failed, and I'm ashamed."

2) Ask one restoration question:
"What is my next right step toward integrity?"

3) Take one repair step (as appropriate):

- confession to a trusted person,
- making amends,
- seeking counsel,
- or choosing a boundary that protects others.

Prayer:

"Jesus, meet me on the shore.
Feed me with mercy.
Restore what can be restored.
Teach me to live forward with humility and truth."

Chapter Twenty-Four

When You Can't See God, Look at Me

This chapter explores Jesus—
for anyone who can't see God in the valley,
and needs to be held by the One who finished the work.

I know what it is to be surrounded by people and still feel alone.

I know what it is to be misunderstood.
To be doubted.
To be praised one day and criticized the next.

I know what it is to carry a mission so heavy it presses into your body.

And I know what it is to walk into suffering with open eyes.

I stepped into your world on purpose.

Not because humanity impressed Me.
Because humanity needed Me.

Not because pain was small.
Because pain was real.

I did not come to watch you struggle from a distance.

I came close.

I learned hunger.
I learned fatigue.
I learned what it means to be interrupted.
I learned what it means to be touched by desperate hands.
I learned what it means to be looked at like a miracle and treated like a threat.

I watched people carry burdens they didn't have language for.

Grief.
Shame.
Fear.
Poverty.
Isolation.
Spiritual confusion.
Bodies that ached.
Minds that spiraled.
Hearts that had learned to brace for disappointment.

I did not step back from them.

I moved toward them.

I touched lepers.
I ate with outcasts.
I spoke gently to the ashamed.
I made room for the weary.

I protected the vulnerable.
I confronted the powerful who used religion as a weapon.

And when people asked, "What is God like?"

I did not answer with a theory.

I answered with My life.

If you want to know what God is like, look at Me.

Look at My hands reaching for the ones who feel untouchable.
Look at My eyes holding the ones who feel unseen.
Look at My voice steadying the ones who feel afraid.
Look at My posture—always turning toward the hurting, not away.

This is what the Father is like.

And then the night came when everything narrowed.

The night before the cross, the air felt heavy.

Not because I didn't trust the Father.
Because I was fully human, carrying what was coming.

I knew betrayal was already moving through the room.
I knew denial would happen before morning.
I knew My friends would fall asleep while My soul

wrestled.
I knew the crowd would choose a criminal over Me.
I knew the nails would not be symbolic.
I knew the silence would feel real.

And still—I stayed.

Not because love is easy.

Because love is faithful.

I went to pray.

Not to escape.
To entrust.

To place My mission back into the Father's hands—not as a surrender of purpose, but as a surrender of control.

I prayed for the ones who had walked with Me.
I prayed for the ones who would carry the message after I was gone.
And I prayed for the ones who would believe later.

I prayed for you.

I asked the Father to keep you.
To guard your heart.
To hold you steady when the world presses in.
To make you one—connected, not isolated.
To let love be the home you live in.

And then I said words that still stand over every valley:

“I have honored You on earth by finishing what You entrusted to Me.”

Do you understand what that means?

It means your salvation is not fragile.

It is not held together by your perfect emotions.
It is not maintained by your flawless behavior.
It is not secured by your ability to “feel” God every day.

It is secured by Me.

There will be seasons when you cannot see God.

Seasons when your prayers feel thin.
Seasons when grief pulls you under.
Seasons when your body becomes the valley.
Seasons when others fail you.
Seasons when you fail yourself.
Seasons when doubt feels louder than faith.
Seasons when the numbers don’t work.
Seasons when you don’t know what to do next.

In those seasons, your story may feel compromised.

You may wonder if you’ve disqualified yourself.
If you’ve ruined what God planned.

If your weakness has undone your relationship with Him.

Listen to Me:

Your story is not ultimately defined by where you have been in these chapters.

It is defined by where you are with Me now.

If you are with Me—reaching, returning, trembling, honest—then you are not lost.

You are held.

I did not complete My work so you would spend your life wondering if the Father tolerates you.

I completed My work so you could know you are loved.

Fully.
Steadily.
Without the constant fear of being cast out.

The cross was not a message of disappointment.

It was a declaration of reconciliation.

I carried humanity's wandering.
I carried shame.
I carried the separation you feel when you think God has moved away.

And I removed what stood between you and the Father.

So when you feel distant, do not assume love has ended.

Sometimes you are exhausted.
Sometimes you are grieving.
Sometimes your nervous system is overwhelmed.
Sometimes you are healing from wounds others caused.
Sometimes you are carrying more than one human heart can hold.

And in those moments, your feelings may go quiet.

But My love does not.

I am not offended by your trembling faith.
I am not threatened by your questions.
I am not surprised by your humanity.

I know what dust feels like.
I know what tears taste like.
I know what it is to ask the Father, "Why?"
I know what it is to surrender the outcome and keep loving.

So come to Me as you are.

Not when you have the perfect prayer.
Not when your emotions are steady.
Not when you've cleaned up every part of your story.

Come now.

If you can only offer one sentence, offer it.

If you can only offer one breath, offer it.

I can carry what you cannot.

And one day—sooner than you think—your valley will end.

There will be a final chapter for you, too.

Not defined by the season that broke you.
Not defined by the failure that embarrassed you.
Not defined by the grief that hollowed you out.

Defined by the Father's welcome.

Defined by reunion.

Defined by a love that finishes what it starts.

That is why I prayed.

That is why I went to the cross.

That is why I rose.

So that when you cannot see God, you can look at Me—and know:

The Father is still holding your hand.

And your story is still being written.

The Gentle Truth

Your life is not ultimately defined by the valleys you have walked through. It is defined by Jesus—by His finished work and His present hold on you.

If you cannot see God, look at Jesus. He is what the Father is like, and He has completed the work that secures your relationship with God.

A Small Practice for the Valley

When you feel distant from God, try this simple practice:

1) Read John 17 slowly, as if you are listening to Jesus pray for you.
2) After each paragraph, pause and whisper: "Hold me."
3) End with one sentence:
"Jesus, define my story by Your love."

Prayer:

"Jesus, when I can't see the Father, help me look at You.
Thank You for finishing the work.
Hold my hand in this chapter.
Lead me home."

Chapter Twenty-Five

There Is No Shame in Being Human

**This chapter explores your humanity—
for anyone who thinks you surprised God,
and needs to know there is always a way forward in His love.**

I want to speak to the part of you that still believes you surprised God.

The part that whispers, "I should be farther along by now."
The part that says, "If I were stronger, I wouldn't be here."
The part that carries quiet shame—not always for what you did, but for who you are in your weakness, your limits, your emotions, your humanity.

This book has walked you through many valleys.

Grief.
Disappointment.
Waiting.
Debt.
Confusion.
Chronic illness.
Church hurt.
Public failure.

Private regret.
Dry seasons where your heart couldn't sing.
Moments when you needed proof.
Days when you didn't know what to do next.

And if you've been listening closely, you've seen something consistent across every story:

Humanity has never taken God off guard.

Not once.

The Bible is not a collection of flawless people who kept it together.

It is a witness to a faithful God who keeps coming close to people who don't.

Hagar ran into the wilderness with an abandoned heart—and God found her.
Martha wrestled with grief and disappointment—and Jesus met her at the tomb.
Sarah laughed at a promise she couldn't imagine—and God kept His word anyway.
Elijah crashed after victory—and God fed him, let him sleep, and spoke gently.
Joseph suffered injustice—and God stayed with him in the pit and in the palace.
The prodigal son made a mess—and mercy ran down the road to meet him.
The widow stared at numbers that didn't work—and

God multiplied what was in her hand.
David went numb, David failed morally, and David lived forward—and God kept shepherding him.
Thomas needed proof—and Jesus came with peace, not shame.
Paul was wounded by the church—and God promised, "I Myself will shepherd you."
Hannah was misunderstood—and God heard her silent prayer.
A woman with a reputation met Jesus at a well—and He told the truth without disgust.
A father waited for a wandering child—and love stayed tender.
Daniel did the right thing and still suffered—and God met him in the den.
Gideon was overwhelmed—and God gave him one step at a time.
Peter failed publicly—and Jesus rebuilt him with breakfast and a calling.
And then Jesus Himself—fully human—walked into suffering with open eyes, completing the work of redemption.

Do you see the thread?

Every one of these stories includes a moment where the human heart drifted or broke.

Not all in the same way.

Some drifted in fear.
Some drifted in fatigue.
Some drifted in grief.
Some drifted in shame.
Some drifted because they couldn't see God clearly anymore.

But none of it left God without a way forward.

Here is one of the most healing truths a believer can carry:

There is never a moment when God has no plan.

We talk about "Plan A" as if God stands helpless when we make a mistake.

But God is never helpless.

He is never cornered by your choices.
He is never shocked by your emotions.
He is never confused by your nervous system.
He is never outpaced by your loss.
He is never without mercy, wisdom, or a path forward.

That doesn't mean your choices don't matter.

They do.

Our wandering is real.
Harm is real.
Consequences are real.

But God's faithfulness is more real.

And the gospel is not the message that humans finally stop being human.

The gospel is the message that God entered humanity and redeemed it.

Jesus came to heal the seasons when we lose our way—when our choices disrupt fellowship, make God feel distant, and knock us off our path.

He did not come to shame you into transformation.

He came to love you into wholeness.

He came to reconcile you to the Father.

So if you are reading this book and feeling the weight of "I should have known better" or "I've ruined too much" or "I can't believe I'm still struggling," I want you to hear this plainly:

You can put your hand in God's hand at any moment and walk forward.

Not when you feel worthy.
Now.

Not when you've repaired every consequence.
Now.

Not when you have the perfect plan.
Now.

Because return is always available.

This is what repentance is—not punishment, not groveling, not self-hatred.

Repentance is turning back toward God and discovering He has not stopped being God.

It is choosing truth.
Choosing humility.
Choosing the next right step.
Choosing to be held.

And when you do, you will discover something that changes how you live:

God is not waiting for you to prove you've learned your lesson before He loves you again.

He loves you because He loves you.

That is who He is.

That is why the final words of Jesus in John 17 matter so much.

On the edge of the cross—on the eve of suffering—Jesus prayed to the Father and said:

"I have honored You on earth by finishing what You entrusted to Me."

Do you know what that means for you?

It means that no valley gets the final word.

Not grief.
Not failure.
Not shame.
Not sickness.
Not fear.
Not confusion.
Not the season where you couldn't feel God.
Not even the chapter where you wandered and got off course.

The final word is Jesus.

And if Jesus is the final word, then your life can still end with faithfulness.

It can still end with peace.

It can still end with that same holy confidence—because your confidence is not in your perfection, but in His finished work.

No matter where you find yourself in this very moment, you can arrive at the end of your life with a heart that says, "Father, I have completed what You gave me to do."

Not because you never struggled.

Because you kept returning.

Because you kept walking with Him—hand in hand—through every valley.

Because you believed love was stronger than your humanity.

And it is.

So let this be your closing reminder:

There is no shame in your humanity.

Your limits do not disqualify you.
Your emotions do not surprise God.
Your setbacks do not cancel your calling.
Your detours do not erase God's faithfulness.

There is always a way forward.

And the way forward has a Name.

When you can't see Him, He still sees you.

When you can't hear Him, He still hears you.

When you're off course, He still knows exactly where you are.

The Gentle Truth

Your humanity does not take God off guard. Scripture is not a record of flawless people, but a witness to a faithful God.

God is never without a way forward. The gospel is not the message that you finally stop being human—it is the message that Jesus redeemed humanity.

A Small Practice for the Valley

Try this "return prayer" practice:

1) Place your hand in your own palm (a physical reminder).
2) Whisper:
"God, I return."

3) Name one next step:
"Today I will ______."

Prayer:

"Father, thank You that my humanity does not surprise You. Thank You that Jesus finished the work. Hold my hand in this chapter. Teach me to walk forward—one faithful step at a time."

Closing Prayer

Father,

Thank You for meeting us in the valleys—when we are grieving, uncertain, overwhelmed, or ashamed. Thank You that our humanity does not surprise You, and that Jesus has completed the work You entrusted Him to do.

Hold our hand in the chapter we are living now. Give us courage for the next step. Restore what has been wounded. And teach us to live forward—one faithful day at a time.

In Jesus' name, amen.

Discussion Guide

Use these questions for personal reflection or group discussion. Choose one or two per sitting if time is limited—these are designed to invite honest conversation, not quick answers.

Chapter 1: Peter — Fear, shame, and mercy that meets you first

1. Where do you see yourself in Peter's fear—what situations make you feel pressured to hide your faith or your true self?

2. What does shame sound like in your inner dialogue, and what would it mean for mercy to meet you before you can explain yourself?

3. What do you notice about Jesus' posture toward Peter—and how does that reshape your view of God's posture toward you?

4. What is one small "return" step you can take this week (confession, honesty, reaching out, prayer)?

5. How can this group/community become a safe place for restoration rather than performance?

Chapter 2: Martha — Grief, disappointment, and waiting for resurrection

1. What part of Martha's story mirrors your grief or disappointment—what "God, if You had…" sentence lives in you?

2. When you are waiting for your own "resurrection," what feels hardest about the in-between?

3. How does Jesus' presence at the tomb speak to the way God meets you in sorrow?

4. What is one practice that helps you grieve without rushing yourself (rest, prayer, walking, journaling, support)?

5. What would hope look like for you this week—small, realistic, and gentle?

Chapter 3: Sarah — Taking matters into your hands and learning to trust

1. Where do you feel tempted to take matters into your own hands right now, and why?

2. What fears or pressures drive that impulse (timeline, comparison, control, insecurity)?

3. What do you learn about God's faithfulness from Sarah's long wait?

4. What is one area where you can practice trust through a concrete step this week?

5. How can we hold space for both honesty and hope in seasons of waiting?

Chapter 4: Hagar — Abandonment, being unseen, and God who finds you

1. When have you felt unseen, displaced, or "outside the room" like Hagar?

2. What would it change for you to believe God finds people in the wilderness—not only in safe places?

3. Where do you need God's naming—His tender recognition of your pain—right now?

4. What is one "wilderness mercy" you can ask for today (help, provision, clarity, companionship)?

5. Who might God be inviting you to see and honor the way He saw Hagar?

Chapter 5: Naomi — Loss, emptiness, and provision on the road

1. What has loss taken from you—identity, future, stability, joy—and how does Naomi's story name that honestly?

2. Where have you felt bitter, numb, or unable to hope, and what do you need from God in that place?

3. What does faithful “walking forward” look like when you don’t feel strong?

4. What is one small step toward provision or support you can take this week (ask, apply, rest, reach out)?

5. How can community help someone rebuild after loss without trying to fix them?

Chapter 6: Job — Suffering without answers and God’s presence

1. What unanswered “why” questions are you carrying right now?

2. How do you tend to respond to suffering—control, withdrawal, anger, spiritual striving, silence?

3. What does it mean to you that God may meet you with presence more than explanations?

4. What would it look like to practice honest prayer without self-censoring this week?

5. What support do you need to endure well—spiritually, emotionally, practically?

Chapter 7: Elijah — Crash after victory and the rhythm of rest

1. Where have you experienced a crash after carrying too much—success, responsibility, ministry, family demands?

2. What does your body signal when you've gone past your limits?

3. What do you learn about God from the way He feeds Elijah, lets him sleep, and speaks gently?

4. What is one boundary or rhythm of rest you can honor this week?

5. How can we normalize rest as obedience—not weakness—in this group/community?

Chapter 8: Joseph — Betrayal, misunderstanding, and redeemed harm

1. Where have you been betrayed or misunderstood, and how has that shaped your trust?

2. What "pit" season are you in right now—what feels unfair or stuck?

3. How does Joseph's story reshape your understanding of God's ability to redeem harm?

4. What is one faithful action you can take even before your circumstances change?

5. Who can you trust with your story in a healthy way as you heal?

Chapter 9: The Prodigal Son — Making a mess and coming home

1. What does "far country" look like in your life—where have you drifted, numbed out, or tried to escape?

2. What keeps you from coming home (shame, fear, pride, consequences, feeling unworthy)?

3. What stands out to you about the Father's mercy, and what does it reveal about God?

4. What would one step toward home look like this week?

5. How can we respond to return with compassion while still honoring truth and accountability?

Chapter 10: The Widow — When the numbers don't work and God multiplies

1. Where are you facing "numbers that don't work"—finances, time, energy, capacity?

2. What emotions come up when you realize you don't have enough?

3. What does God's multiplication in the widow's story teach you about provision and partnership?

4. What is onc "small thing in your hand" you can offer God this week?

5. What practical support might God be inviting you to receive from others?

Chapter 11: David — Spiritual numbness and honest faith

1. What does spiritual numbness look like for you—what symptoms show up (apathy, fatigue, disconnect, irritability)?

2. What do you assume God thinks about you when you can't feel Him?

3. How does David's honesty invite you to tell the truth without shame?

4. What is one gentle spiritual rhythm you can keep even when you feel numb?

5. What helps you stay connected to God without forcing emotions?

Chapter 12: David — Moral failure, repentance, and restoration

1. When have you crossed a line that caused regret—what do you fear it means about your future?

2. What is the difference between conviction that leads to life and shame that keeps you stuck?

3. What do you learn about God from David's repentance and restoration?

4. What is one repair step you can take (as appropriate): confession, amends, counsel, boundaries?

5. How can this group hold both grace and truth when someone has failed?

Chapter 13: David — Successes, setbacks, and living forward

1. Where have you seen God use you well—what victories or faithfulness do you remember?

2. How have past numbness or failure tried to rewrite your identity or disqualify you?

3. What do you learn from David's whole story about living forward with God?

4. What is one present-tense step toward your future that you've been avoiding?

5. What would it look like to let God define you by belovedness rather than your worst chapter?

Chapter 14: Thomas — Doubt, needing proof, and peace

1. What questions or doubts feel most honest for you right now?

2. In what ways might doubt be grief, fear, or overwhelm trying to protect you?

3. What stands out about how Jesus meets Thomas—what does that show you about God?

4. What does "stay within reach" look like for you this week?

5. How can we be a community where questions are welcomed and faith can grow gently?

Chapter 15: Paul — Church hurt and the Shepherd who cares personally

1. What kind of church hurt have you experienced, and what has it done to your trust?

2. How have you tangled God's character with the actions of people who misrepresented Him?

3. What does Ezekiel 34 mean to you—how does it feel to hear God say, "I Myself will shepherd you"?

4. What boundaries or healing steps do you need in order to rebuild trust safely?

5. What would healthy spiritual community look like for you going forward?

Chapter 16: The Woman Who Suffered Twelve Years — Chronic illness and dignity

1. How has ongoing illness/pain/fatigue affected your identity, relationships, or faith?

2. What does it feel like when your body becomes the valley—what do you miss most about "normal"?

3. What do you learn from Jesus calling her "Daughter" before anything else?

4. What is one compassionate way you can care for your body this week without guilt?

5. Where do you need peace—not just relief—in your current season?

Chapter 17: Ruth — Caregiving, exhaustion, and daily bread

1. Who are you carrying right now, and what is it costing you emotionally or physically?

2. Where do you feel like you are disappearing because you are always needed?

3. What do you learn about God's care for caregivers through Ruth's story?

4. What help can you ask for this week (one specific request)?

5. What boundaries or rhythms would protect your tenderness while you keep loving?

Chapter 18: Hannah — Misunderstood grief and silent prayer

1. When have you been misunderstood—especially when you were already hurting?

2. What do you tend to do when someone misreads you (withdraw, defend, people-please, go silent)?

3. What does it mean to you that God heard Hannah's prayer even when others judged her?

4. What truth do you need to name out loud this week to protect your dignity?

5. Who is a safe person you can share your real heart with right now?

Chapter 19: The Samaritan Woman — Reputation, shame, and living water

1. What labels or reputations have you carried—fair or unfair—and how have they shaped you?

2. What "heat of the day" places do you avoid because of shame or fear of being seen?

3. What stands out about Jesus telling the truth without disgust?

4. What would living water look like for you—what thirst are you trying to satisfy?

5. What is one step toward honesty, healing, or community you can take this week?

Chapter 20: The Waiting Father — Loving someone you can't control

1. Who do you love that you cannot control, and what does waiting feel like in your body and mind?

2. What is the difference between wise love and enabling love in your situation?

3. What do you learn about God's heart from the father who runs to meet return?

4. What boundary or self-care step do you need so waiting doesn't consume you?

5. How can we pray for those we love without turning prayer into control?

Chapter 21: Daniel — Injustice and faithfulness under pressure

1. Where has doing the right thing still cost you—what feels unfair about your situation?

2. What has injustice tempted you to become (bitter, cynical, anxious, resigned)?

3. What helps you most: God changing outcomes or God sustaining you with presence—and why?

4. What is one next right step you can take while justice feels delayed?

5. What support do you need so integrity doesn't become isolation?

Chapter 22: Gideon — Overwhelm, indecision, and the next step

1. Where are you stuck right now—what decision feels impossible to make?

2. What fears are underneath the indecision (failure, loss, mishearing God, disappointing others)?

3. What do you learn from God's patience with Gideon and His "one step at a time" leadership?

4. What is one small step you can take in the next 24 hours toward clarity?

5. How can we hold space for slow discernment without shame in this group/community?

Chapter 23: Peter — Public failure and rebuilding trust

1. What does your "public failure" story look like—where do you feel exposed or disqualified?

2. What do you believe God thinks about you in that place, and where did you learn that belief?

3. What stands out about Jesus feeding Peter before restoring him?

4. What is one repair or integrity step God may be inviting you to take this week?

5. What would restoration look like that is both gracious and responsible?

Chapter 24: Jesus — Seeing God through the finished work

1. When you cannot see God, what do you usually assume—and how does Jesus reframe that?

2. What line or image from John 17 (or this chapter) feels most personal to you right now?

3. What does it mean that your relationship with God is secured by Jesus' finished work?

4. What would it look like to let Jesus define your story in this season?

5. How can we practice seeing God through Jesus together—especially in hard weeks?

Chapter 25: Humanity — No shame, always a way forward

1. Where do you feel ashamed of being human—limits, emotions, setbacks, detours?

2. Which story in this book most convinced you that humanity does not take God off guard?

3. What does “God is never without a way forward” mean for your current chapter?

4. What is one hand-in-hand step you will take with God this week?

5. What do you hope your life will be able to say at the end—echoing John 17: “I honored You by finishing what You entrusted to me”?

About the Author

Cindy H. Carr, D.Min., MACL, is an author, pastor, and pastoral counselor who was deeply shaped by contemplative engagement with Scripture during her seminary experience at Eastern Mennonite Seminary.

She is passionate about helping readers move beyond studying the Bible solely for information and into encountering it for formation—entering the story to experience the heart of God.

Cindy credits Wendy J. Miller—her campus pastor, professor, and lifelong mentor—for teaching her how to enter into Scripture not only for knowledge, but for experience.

That approach transformed Cindy's walk with God, and she now shares it with others who long to engage Scripture in the same way.

Learn more about Cindy and her work at
CindyHCarr.com

www.ingramcontent.com/pod-product-compliance
Lightning Source LLC
LaVergne TN
LVHW010650110826
845149LV00014B/3011

* 9 7 8 1 9 7 1 1 9 2 2 3 9 *